Praise for *The Mi*

Betty Kovács gives us not just one but two messages that are vital for our lives and times. First, that our individual mortality is an illusion, for death and birth are a cycle through which life, the sole reality, continues transformed, but unbroken. Two, that as more and more people are turning inward and experiencing the true dimensions of their inner self, a new consciousness is being born on this planet–a consciousness that we are all part of each other and of the cosmos, and that together we can heal the Earth–that we can dance, as Betty Kovács says, the Round Dance. Few things could be more important for us both individually and collectively than understanding these messages.

—Ervin László, Ph.D. Author, Systems Theorist, Founder of The Club of Budapest, twice Nobel Peace Prize nominee

The Miracle of Death is an inspiring, sensitively told story, opening the door for our whole culture to a new way of living.

—Anne Baring, Jungian analyst and author and co-author of seven books, including *The Dream of the Cosmos: A Quest for the Soul, The Myth of the Goddess: Evolution of an Image* (with Jules Cashford) and *Soul Power* (with Dr. Scilla Elworthy)

The Miracle of Death is an interweaving of the story of a profound loss of a child...and at once a remarkable insight into the mystical experience of that mystery. Dr. Kovács brings in both ancient and modern philosophy and spiritual teaching together with her own visions and insights and shows us not only how we can better cope with death of a child or loved one, but, because of it, find the opportunity to profoundly change our whole world view. Readers will find this both deeply moving and clearly informative.

—Fred Alan Wolf, Ph.D. Theoretical Physicist, National Book Award-winning author of *Matter into Feeling, Mind into Matter, The Spiritual Universe, Taking the Quantum Leap,* and *Time Loops and Space Twists*

The Miracle of Death tells the poignant story of a couple whose only son, killed in an automobile accident, seemed to start communicating with them through dreams and visions. Its readers will formulate their own opinions regarding the messages received, but can not help to be moved by the provocative insights they contain. This book describes nothing less than the very nature of existence, and provides a remarkable blueprint for coping with the challenges posed by the 21st century.

—Stanley Krippner, Ph.D. Co-author, *Personal Mythology*

Dr. Kovács' personal journey is supported by the latest research on precognitive dreams and survival of consciousness after death. *The Miracle of Death* is an inspired and inspiring book.

—Gary E. Schwartz, Ph.D. Professor of Psychology, Surgery, Medicine, Neurology, and Psychiatry, Co-author, *The Afterlife Experiments* and *The Living Energy Universe*

Dr. Kovács has joined the growing ranks of academic, medical, and scientific professionals who are researching and exploring the capacities of the human mind. Her experiences and conclusions pose a giant step forward in understanding ourselves and the mysteries of other dimensions. You will be moved by her personal loss, insights, discoveries, and conclusion that "Love and life are indestructible." This is a book you *need* to read.

—Joel Martin, Co-author, *Love Beyond Life* and National Bestseller *We Don't Die*

This is much more than a book about death, it is a book about life and a powerful call to connect with deeper orders of reality, to live our lives as consciously as possible, and to play our part in the healing of humanity and of the earth.

—David Lorimer, *Network: The Scientific and Medical Network Review Magazine* (UK), Director of The Scientific and Medical Network (1986-2000), Programme Director, author and editor of over a dozen books

THE MIRACLE *of* DEATH

THERE IS NOTHING BUT LIFE

TO EXPERIENCE THIS ESSENTIAL TRUTH
IS TO EXPERIENCE THE MIRACLE
OF DEATH

Betty J. Kovács

Betty J. Kovács, Ph.D.

Foreword by Anne Baring

Claremont, California

The Miracle of Death
by Betty J. Kovács, Ph.D.

Published by: The Kamlak Center
112 Harvard Avenue #23
Claremont, California 91711-4716
Website: www.kamlak.com

Copyright © 2020 by The Kamlak Center

All rights reserved. This publication may not be reproduced, stored in a retrieval system, or transmitted in whole or in part, in any form or by any means, electronic, mechanical, photocopying, recording, or otherwise without the prior written permission of the publisher except in the case of brief quotations. For further information write to the publisher or visit www.kamlak.com.

Cover Art: Robert Lentz
Cover Design by Carl D. Galian

ISBN: 978-0-9721005-3-3 Hard cover
ISBN: 978-0-9721005-0-2 Soft cover
ISBN: 978-0-9721005-4-0 Ebook

Publisher's Cataloging-In-Publication Data
(Prepared by The Donohue Group, Inc.)

Names: Kovács, Betty J., author. | Baring, Anne, 1931- writer of supplementary textual content.
Title: The miracle of death : there is nothing but life / Betty J. Kovács, Ph.D. ; foreword by Anne Baring.
Description: Claremont, California : The Kamlak Center, [2020] | "To experience this essential truth is to experience the miracle of death." | Includes bibliographical references and index.
Identifiers: ISBN 9780972100533 (hard cover) | ISBN 9780972100502 (soft cover) | ISBN 9780972100540 (ebook)
Subjects: LCSH: Death--Psychological aspects. | Kovács, Betty J.-- Family. | Spiritualism. | Future life. | Grief.
Classification: LCC BF789.D4 K63 2020 (print) | LCC BF789.D4 (ebook) | DDC 155.937--dc23

Printed in the United States of America

Grateful acknowledgment is made to all copyright holders for permission to reprint previously published material contained in this work.

The author and publisher acknowledge permission to reprint the following excerpts:

Excerpt from *Witchcraze: A New History of the European Witch Hunts* by Anne Llewellyn Barstow. Copyright © 1994 by Anne Llewellyn Barstow. Reprinted by permission of Harper Collins Publishers Inc.

Excerpt from *Essays on a Science of Mythology: The Myths of the Divine Child and the Divine Maiden* by C.G. Jung and C. Kerényi. Copyright © 1963 by Princeton University Press. Reprinted by permission of Princeton University Press.

Excerpt from *The Politics of Experience* by R.D. Laing. Copyright © 1967 by R.D. Laing. Reproduced by permission of Penguin Books Ltd.

Excerpt from "The Gospel of Thomas" from *The Nag Hammadi Library in English,* 3rd Completely Revised Ed. by James M. Robinson, General Editor. Copyright © 1978, 1988 by E.J. Brill, Leiden, The Netherlands. Reprinted by permission of Harper Collins Publishers Inc.

Excerpt from *When Women Were Priests: Women's Leadership in the Early Church and the Scandal of their Subordination in the Rise of Christianity* by Karen Jo Torjesen. Copyright © 1993 by Karen Jo Torjesen. Reprinted by permission of Harper Collins Publishers Inc.

Excerpt from *The Egyptian Mysteries* by Arthur Versluis. Copyright © 1988 by Arthur Versluis. Reproduced by permission of Penguin Books Ltd.

~

Every effort has been made to trace copyright holders for the following publications. The publisher is willing to rectify any omissions in future editions.

Fry, Christopher. "Comedy," *Comedy: Meaning and Form*. Edited by Robert W. Corrigan. San Francisco: Chandler Publishing Company, 1965.

Laing, R.D. *The Politics of Experience*. New York: Pantheon Books, 1967. (Copyright holder for United States territories.)

Schwaller de Lubicz, R.A. *Symbol and the Symbolic: Egypt, Science and the Evolution of Consciousness*. Translated by Robert and Deborah Lawlor. Brookline: Autumn Press/Random House, Inc., 1978.

Stace, Walter T., editor. *The Teachings of the Mystics: Selections from the Great Mystics and Mystical Writings of the World*. New York: Mentor Books/The New American Library of World Literature, Inc., 1960.

Strömberg, Gustaf. *The Soul of the Universe*. North Hollywood: Educational Research Institute, 1965.

~

Cover Art "Compassion Mandala." Copyright © 1989 by Robert Lentz. Image courtesy of Trinity Stores. www.trinitystores.com.

Jacket Design by Douglas Paul Designs.

Design Consultant Humberto Narro.

Page Design by One-On-One Book Production, West Hills, California.

DISCLAIMER

All the stories in this book are true. Each person reviewed the account of his or her story, and each living subject has signed a legal release. Neither Betty J. Kovács nor The Kamlak Center shall have liability or responsibility to any person or entity with respect to any loss or damage caused, or alleged to have been caused, directly or indirectly, by the information in this book. If you do not agree to be bound by the above, you may return this book to the publisher for a full refund.

A MIRACLE is an event that **appears** *to contradict the known laws of science. Such events are always taking place around us, in us, and throughout this infinitely creative universe. No science, however advanced, could possibly include all the laws of creativity.*

~

"The most beautiful thing we can experience is the mysterious. It is the source of all true art and science."

~ Albert Einstein

"The world would have you agree with its dismal dream of limitation. But the light would have you soar like the eagle of your sacred visions."

~ Alan Cohen

"Every person's life is a sacred text."

~ Novalis

To the Bard

Let the Bard in each of us ignite artistic consciousness,
create new angles of perceiving reality, and
inspire the Round Dance of infinite possibilities.

ACKNOWLEDGMENTS

I would like to thank my friends, students, and colleagues who have taken the time to read and discuss with me this work in progress. My sincere gratitude goes to my friend and colleague Margaret Marsh for having read the manuscript with an eagle's eye and an open mind. Her valuable insights have made a definite difference in this project.

Special thanks to Dustin and Jenny Ladd, Conrad and Vickie Taylor, and Woody and Claudia Aplanalp for their friendship and trust. I applaud Jenny for her mature and courageous response to life and all these young people for their passion to create a better world. As teenagers Pisti and his friends longed for a world in which each person's purpose and creativity could be realized. Over the years the young people in Pisti's circle of friends shared stories with me that have deeply influenced my work and have surely enriched my life. Thank you all for sharing a bit of the extraordinary with me.

I am grateful to my extended family for their love and support throughout this journey: my nieces Lisa Rogers and Linda Dye; my brother-in-law Paul Kovács, his wife and my good friend Adel; my Hungarian family, including my nephew Tibi with whom I spent many hours in conversation and laughter while he was in America; my European "daughters" Brigitta Marx Hirai and Anita Nagypál; and Jenny's parents Phyllis and Bob Horn. Thanks to my dear friends Jackie and Jack Sullivan who checked on me every day and with whom I ate so many meals that our parting words became "until we eat again." And thanks to Maria Andrade for the years of friendship that we shared. Special thanks to the faculty, staff, and students at Pasadena City College and the members of the Jung Society of Claremont. I will always cherish the incredible stories surrounding death that many of you have shared with me over the years. My deep gratitude to Suzanne Camp and Eetla Soracco for their multidimensional work with Pisti. And to the many others who are not named here, thank you for your enduring love and friendship.

There is simply no way to thank adequately my friend and editor Kimberly Saavedra. From the beginning she was committed to the project. She immediately understood the significance of the visionary experiences and was convinced that they had to be shared with a larger audience. Her intelligence, editorial expertise, and emotional support have fortified the foundation from which I have been able to write *The Miracle of Death.*

I am one of many who have benefitted from the struggle of the indigenous peoples of the Americas to keep the Dream of the Earth alive. I have also been nurtured by the complementary spiritual traditions in Western and Eastern cultures that helped to preserve this Great Mystery. To the degree that *The Miracle of Death* contributes to the awareness of this deep spiritual heritage and aids in our present struggle to collectively awaken to a higher state of consciousness, I will have fulfilled my intention in writing this book.

Contents

Foreword

BY
ANNE BARING

There is a beautiful passage by an anonymous writer of another age that is sometimes read at the end of a funeral service: "For life is eternal and love is immortal and death is only an horizon, and an horizon is nothing save the limit of our sight."

The passionate longing of the human heart has always been to press beyond the boundaries of the known, to break through the limitations of our understanding. This is perhaps our most fundamental and essential freedom. Now, more than ever, we need to honor that longing and welcome those pioneers who can unveil new horizons, new possibilities of understanding our nature, our potential and our destiny.

This moving, courageous book, written with great sensitivity and intelligence and forged in the fiery crucible of personal experience, bears witness to the fact that there is only Life beyond death, that there is nothing *but* Life. Its powerful and compelling story, rich in insight, wisdom and astonishing revelation, offers us a new understanding of ourselves and our unacknowledged needs that can carry us beyond the present limit of our sight.

The inevitability of death has weighed like a stone on the human heart. So much fear, grief, anger and emotional pain have been associated with it. The greatest sorrow, the greatest fear we can experience in our lives is the loss of a beloved parent, child or companion, believing that he or she is lost to us forever. *The Miracle of Death* is a story that can reach into our hearts and undo the spell of that sorrow, that fear, that loss; its healing power can loosen the grip of our fear of death. It can awaken us to awareness of something that was once *instinctively* known and has long been forgotten—that we participate in and are contained by the creative consciousness and loving intelligence of the universe. Whatever name we give this consciousness—whether God, or Universal Mind, or Energy, or Spirit—does not really matter. What matters is that we recognize the existence of a dimension of reality beyond the one we know and enter into a relationship with it. This book offers us a template of how to increase our awareness of our connection to that dimension.

It is extraordinary that, with all the vast amount of information we have available to us, we still know so little about the two most numinous experiences of our lives—our birth and our death. From what other level of reality do we come at our birth? And to what other level do we go when we die? Even more extraordinary is the fact that science, until very recently, has not taken seriously the huge amount of material gathered over the past hundred or so years by institutions devoted to recording non-ordinary experiences (near-death experiences) as well as communications to the living from the "dead." Nor has it accepted as worthy of scientific attention the experience of visionaries and mystics of all cultures and times that has testified to the existence of that other dimension of reality and the possibility of a direct relationship with it.

Astonishing discoveries have been made about the nature of consciousness by such outstanding individuals as C.G. Jung and Stanislav Grof; many individuals have communicated their out-of-the-body and near-death experiences; but the implications of all this material have not been given serious consideration. Christopher Bache comments on this in his book *Dark Night, Early Dawn*: "Western thought has committed itself to a vision of reality that is based almost entirely on the daylight world of ordinary states of consciousness while systematically ignoring the knowledge that can be gained from the nighttime sky of nonordinary states.... Trapped within the horizon of the near-at-hand, our culture creates myths about the unreliability and irrelevance of nonordinary states. Meanwhile, our social fragmentation continues to deepen, reflecting in part our inability to answer the most basic existential questions."[1]

The neglect of a vitally significant field of human experience has meant that the experiences and discoveries related to this field are considered to be irrelevant or worse, symptoms of deluded minds. However, the growing pressure of current experiential evidence, most importantly in the field of transpersonal psychology and psychedelic research but also in the work of scientists at the cutting edge of physics and cosmology, suggests that we are poised at the threshold of a breakthrough—a revelation in our understanding of the nature of reality.

William James's carefully chosen words, written a hundred years ago, seem more relevant than ever today: "Our normal waking consciousness, rational consciousness as we call it, is but one special type of consciousness, whilst all about it, parted from it by the filmiest of screens, there lie potential forms of consciousness entirely different. We may go through life without suspecting their existence; but apply the requisite stimulus, and at a touch they are there in all their completeness, definite types of mentality which probably somewhere have their field of application and adaptation. No account of the universe in its totality can be final which leaves these other forms of consciousness quite disregarded."[2]

We no longer have access to other levels or modes of consciousness because our "rational" mind has, over the last four centuries, increasingly ridiculed, disparaged and repressed what it has been unable, so far, to accept, prove or comprehend. It has therefore cut us off from those deeper aspects of our nature that have the power to connect us with other dimensions of reality. Our understanding of life and the interconnectedness of all aspects of it is tragically deficient. As Betty Kovács says, "Our major cultural myth has been one of disconnection, loss, purposelessness, and insignificance. Is there any wonder that we hurt ourselves, each other, our children, and our planet? All life is in danger when we hold a worldview that is not *inclusive*. We know this, yet we fear change and transformation. We fear losing the only reality we know when, truly, only the limitation of that reality is threatened."

This denial has left an aching void in many people's lives that neither religious belief nor scientific progress nor improving the material circumstances of our lives can fill although they are presented as offering all that is necessary to alleviate the suffering of the human condition. What is missing is a sense of our intimate and joyous interaction with an invisible dimension, knowledge of how the relationship with this dimension can be cultivated and how fear can ultimately be replaced by trust. There have been many great teachers, astronauts of the soul, who have pointed the way to a direct experience of reality but their message and their teaching have, for the most part, been misinterpreted or ignored. Belief and its dark companion, fanaticism, have become a substitute for that mysterious relationship.

The story told in this book is so instructive and inspirational because it shows how difficult it is for the academically trained mind to accept the idea of life beyond death and how it repeatedly denies us access to those deeper-dwelling faculties in us that have been repressed and neglected for centuries and have therefore atrophied for want of use. From the denial and repression of these intuitive, creative and imaginative aspects of ourselves have come our materialist belief system and the culture of escalating violence which now threaten us with the disintegration of civilization and, ultimately, with the possible extinction of our species.

As we have become increasingly cut off from these faculties, so, in our relationships with others, we have become increasingly gripped by fear and the need for control, responding to difficult situations with a paranoid defense against our "enemies," ascribing all "good" to ourselves and all "evil" to them. Setting out to eliminate evil by force, we create violence and invite violence in retaliation, creating unbearable suffering and despair for millions. Yet the root of all this lies in our own fragmented psyche and our abysmal ignorance of the oneness and sacredness of life.

What Betty Kovács tells us in clear, vivid imagery is how the deep ground of spirit speaks; how it attracts us to itself and tries to gain our attention; the language and imagery and methods of communication it uses. She shows the importance of paying close attention to dreams, visions, synchronicities and to those often subliminal images that appear fleetingly on the screen of consciousness. She tells how, out of a sustained meditative attention, there was born in her not only a deeper capacity for insight but the opening of her awareness to "a dimension so vast that I was stunned to realize how excruciatingly small a space I had been trained to live in and call reality." What she experienced as her awareness of this dimension expanded was the shattering of the myth of materialism which condemns so many to a meaningless life of "mediocrity, addiction, violence, indifference and fanaticism."

"In our amnesia," she writes, we have "'forgotten' ourselves into a 'terrible dream' where neither mother nor child is nurtured. How had we fallen into this amnesia? How had we lost our self-esteem? How had we lost the understanding that our ego was to be the mirror of our inner uniqueness flowing out of universal Mind? How had we turned this ego 'wrong-side out' so that it had to go snatching and grabbing from the outer world anything that would make us feel good about ourselves? And how had we been able to forget the creative power in every thought and feeling and longing?"

Her message is one of hope and trust that, working together, we will be able to open ourselves to the experience of the mysteries of the universe and weave these mysteries into our daily lives, so healing the deep fragmentation in our nature. On the last page of her book she writes, "As we reconnect, full circle, to the roots of our existence in the Mind of the universe,...we experience the deep unity of birth and death, and we experience the radical creativity of both. We understand that 'Death is as Divine as Life,' because it *is* Life—because 'There is nothing *but* Life.'"

---

1. Christopher Bache, *Dark Night, Early Dawn*, p. 5. Suny Press, Albany, 2000.

2. William James, *The Varieties of Religious Experience*, p. 388. Longmans Green & Co., New York, 1929.

Anne Baring, Ph.D. (Hons)
Winchester, England

M.A., University of Oxford. Honorary Degree of Doctor of Philosophy in Wisdom Studies, Ubiquity University, The Wisdom School. A Jungian analyst and author and co-author of seven books, including *The Myth of the Goddess: Evolution of an Image* (1991) with Jules Cashford; *Soul Power* (2009) with Dr. Scilla Elworthy; and her most recent book, *The Dream of the Cosmos: A Quest for the Soul* (2013). Her website is www.annebaring.com.

Introduction

Death is the fundamental mystery of life, just as life is the fundamental mystery of death.

I

It is not possible to experience one without experiencing the other, but it is possible to be born and to die without participating in the mystery of either. When we do not participate in this mystery, it is usually because we hold a worldview that there is no mystery to experience. Such a worldview has been part of the heritage of Western culture, but now, within this same culture, there is emerging a new "wave of organization"[1] that is radically transforming that worldview.

Traditionally, Western consciousness has nurtured a belief in the superiority of the rational mind and the inferiority of all other mental functions. Instead of recognizing the value of our older brain components in providing us with different modes of knowing, we considered them no longer useful to the rational mind. Thus we excluded their participation in our construction of reality. In so doing, we severed rationality from its roots and denied ourselves access to the wholeness of our own minds.

Carl Sagan understood that "the hallmark of a successful, long-lived civilization may be the ability to achieve a lasting peace among the several brain components."[2] A crucial tool in achieving and maintaining this peace is symbolic, mythic language because it has the capacity to communicate with and activate all of the various components of the mind. It is our first language, the language of the sensuous world, of instinct, of feeling, of memory, of dreams and visions. It is the language of concrete images that can awaken us to the multifaceted nature of inner and outer realities. And it is the language of myth: every culture has symbolic stories it tells itself about itself and its place in the universe. These cultural myths reflect our thought systems and our belief systems. They reveal much about who we are and the choices we make. Thus they mirror back to us our willingness to subscribe to limitation or to claim our potential creativity.

Giambattista Vico, a major theorist of symbolic, mythic language, realized as early as 1725 that even though this language of images develops before rational, conceptual language, it is not irrational. It possesses a poetic logic that forms the roots of logical, conceptual thinking. Yet symbolic language exists in and of itself as a fully developed form of language, as does the idea or conceptual language.[3]

For the whole mind to be captivated and engaged in our perception and conception of reality, we must allow both symbolic language and conceptual language the dignity and respect of equal positions where neither language can control, dominate, or exclude the other. The healthy brain requires that we value our dreams, our life stories, our visions, and our feelings as much as we value our ability to think about ideas. This foundation of equality and respect allows the development of a creative relationship between the symbol and the idea.[4] Once this equal, balanced relationship exists, the mind is free to participate in multiple levels of reality.

But there is more. The mind is also capable of experiencing the *unity* of all levels of reality. This state of consciousness or "state of being" traditionally has been called the mystical experience. This is experienced outside the symbolic and conceptual functions of the mind. In the words of the late Walter T. Stace of Princeton University, mysticism, in its fully developed form, is the experience of "*an ultimate nonsensuous unity in all things,* a oneness or a One to which neither the senses nor the reason can penetrate. In other words, it entirely transcends our sensory-intellectual consciousness." It is that leap of the mind beyond all the polarities of our experience in time and space. "This is a complete paradox. The paradox is not that there is an emptiness *and* a fullness, a darkness *and* a light. The paradox is that the emptiness *is* the fullness, the fullness the emptiness; the darkness *is* the light, the light the darkness."[5]

Some definitions of this experience include sensuous and conceptual elements as long as the unity of self and Other is the core experience. In spite of the fact that this state of being has been experienced by healthy people throughout the world, Western culture also excluded this potential of the mind from its construction of reality. This is understandable from a purely rational perspective: any mental state outside our known forms of logic can appear delusional or pathological.

A larger, more inclusive perspective, however, is now proposed by scientists who are using new technology to explore meditative and mystical experiences. The late Eugene d'Aquili, a psychiatrist and anthropologist, and Andrew Newberg, a neuroscientist, are among those who have explored these mental states by using "advanced imaging techniques" to scan the brain activity of persons experiencing these extraordinary states of consciousness. This research has allowed Newberg to state that "mystical experience is biologically, observably, and scientifically real."[6]

This same brain research has also brought a scientific perspective to the mind's symbolic function—to dreams, mythic narratives, visions, and rituals. These structures, states Newberg, reflect the very nature of the mind "to analyze the perceptions processed by the brain and transform them into a world full of meaning and purpose." It is the mind itself, he continues, that has compelled us "in every culture and throughout time, to seek answers to our most troubling problems in myth." In fact, it is these symbolic, mythic structures that trigger "the neurological mechanisms that can unlock the deepest spiritual potentials of the human mind." There is also growing evidence that the rhythmic, repetitive quality of ritualistic structures stimulates a neurobiological response that can result in expanded consciousness.[7]

According to Newberg, these experiences, from intensified consciousness to mystical consciousness, cannot be dismissed as "'mere' neurological activities" unless we are also willing to dismiss *all* of our "brain's perceptions of the material world." In other words, if we trust the brain's ability to communicate to us what is real in the physical world, there is "no rational reason" to distrust its communication that mystical experience is real.[8]

If it is true that the telling of our stories, dreams, and myths, whether in narrative, gesture, dance, poetry, drama, or ritual, can transform our consciousness by triggering "the neurological mechanisms that can unlock the deepest spiritual potentials of the human mind," then how does the mind respond to what appears to be the end of all potential—the perception of its own death? The answer to this question depends entirely on which function of the mind is responding. The symbolic, mythic and mystical dimensions of the mind respond to death, not as an end, but as a transformation. From this perspective we are able to experience the Great Mystery: death is the source of all life.

But the rational mind has a different response: from this perspective physical death is the end of all we have ever known and loved. This is understandable because the rational mind requires a rational resolution that can be scientifically verified. Without this proof, the only acceptable position has been that death is an end. Since Western culture has excluded resolutions offered by the symbolic, mythic and mystical dimensions of consciousness, we are left with the sorrow of this finality. Thus death has remained the source of our greatest suffering.

This is changing: within science a radical new worldview of an "eternal, living, and evolving" universe is emerging. These are the words of scientists Gary E.R. Schwartz and Linda G.S. Russek. While a professor at Yale University, Schwartz began to explore the hypothesis that "all natural systems store information in an integrative and dynamic fashion that make them alive and evolving." This hypothesis, says Schwartz, "implied not only that all systems were 'alive,' but also that this information [memory] continued as a living, evolving system after the physical structure had deconstructed."[9] As such theories are further explored and developed, the rational mind may yet receive the long awaited conceptual resolution to its perception of death as an end.

Yet even this will not be enough because the *whole* mind needs both the idea *and* the experience. It is our longing to *experience* this "eternal, living, and evolving" universe that calls forth the Great Bard of the symbolic, mythic mind. His* work is to release us from the limits of conceptual thinking and to create new angles of perceiving and experiencing reality. He offers us the gift of knowledge beyond books. He sings to us, he dances, and he tells us stories. His very presence energizes us as his artistic forms restructure space and time. We feel his music in our bones, and when someone asks us about death and life, we too begin to dance, to speak in poetry, to tell stories.

Unfortunately, Western culture has rejected and repressed the gifts of this Bard for so long that we have limited, at least temporarily, our access to this creative potential within the mind. We know that repression produces fear, methods of control, violence, and thus displacement of creative energy. By dismissing the Bard and denying the validity of the symbolic, mythic mind, we lose our connection to the sensuous world, to our bodies, to feeling and memory—and we sever ourselves from the power of empathy and love. We also abandon our evolutionary heritage to participate in multidimensional and mystical realities. Thus we create by default a world in which we cannot create to our fullest potential.

The destructive forces unleashed by this repression form the dark underside of our present worldview. These forces not only thwart our creativity but they persistently threaten what we have already achieved, such as respect for the principles of equality, freedom, and justice. Every individual is creative, but no one creates alone. We are so interrelated and interconnected that the thoughts and actions of each of us affect everyone. When our thoughts and actions cause others to suffer the effects of our dark side, not only do we injure them but we destroy the creativity within ourselves.

---

* The inner Bard may assume any form. I am using the masculine form here because the Bard appeared to me in the forms of my son and the Egyptian god Anubis.

All life is in danger when we hold a worldview that is not *inclusive.* We know this, yet we fear change and transformation. And it is this *fear* and the *belief in our limitations* that prevent us from knowing who we are. In our mostly unconscious effort to maintain our collectively constructed model of reality, we often refuse to validate viable evidence, and we often condemn those who dare to explore these excluded realities. We fear losing the only reality we know when, truly, only the limitation of that reality is threatened.

Today, however, our worldview is changing because millions of people are daring to go beyond this fear and our cultural belief in limitation.[10] Consciousness is undergoing a transformation so powerful that it requires the participation of the whole mind. It is to be expected that we in the West would know very little about such participation or how to activate the denied and rejected modes of knowing. Many ancient cultures, however, did develop techniques to open the mind to these functions, such as meditation, ritual, music, poetry, dance, physical deprivation, isolation, fasting, sacred plants and herbs, specific body postures, various types of physical training, breathing exercises, fragrances, sound, tonal chanting, and the use of symbols, images, and myths. In recent decades there has been renewed interest in the cross-cultural study of these techniques. Since neuroscience is developing an understanding of the symbolic, mythic and mystical dimensions of the mind, perhaps additional research on these and other techniques will follow.

As each of us begins to awaken to our own unique roles within this transformation, we will be in for some real surprises—not only about the vastness and creativity of our new reality but also about our own identity. Our major cultural myth has been one of disconnection, loss, purposelessness, and insignificance. Is there any wonder that we hurt ourselves, each other, our children, and our planet? And is there any wonder that millions of people throughout the world in every walk of life and in every field of research have seen enough suffering and are committed to changing this worldview?

Much of this book is about my own struggle to wake up. I knew that the keys to experiencing "the deepest spiritual potentials" of life were to be found in the symbolic, mythic and mystical dimensions of my mind. This meant that I had to learn to trust my mind's ability to communicate what is real and to free me from the limitations of my Western worldview. Therefore, when I finished my doctoral work in comparative literature and symbolic, mythic language, I realized that I could not consider that scholarship complete. I needed experience, so I had to learn more about those techniques that could activate the functions of my mind that had been denigrated and excluded by my culture. I began to work with people from cultures in which some of these techniques are still practiced. I discovered that a few of the methods offer immediate experience while others require years of discipline, but all of them require patience, balance, caution, reason, compassion, and a commitment to integrated wholeness. I also discovered, as have others before me, that of the techniques explored, each is able to open us, to a greater or lesser degree, to the same multidimensional and mystical realities.

Yet the core experience of the book is the stark reality of the death of all those I loved most in the world. For it was death—that fundamental mystery of life—that truly opened me to a vast and loving universe. The Great Bard did appear. He sang songs and he told me stories about the mysteries of death and life. His presence energized my emptiness and restructured space and time. And gradually I too began to dance, to sing, to tell stories.

II

The symbolic material in this book, the dreams, precognitive experiences, synchronistic events, and waking visions, flooded into our lives during a ten-year period from 1991 to 2001, from the death of our son to the completion of this book. However, during the two years prior to 1991, my husband, our son, and I experienced dreams and visions that, we later realized, helped to prepare us for the events to come. There were two earlier dreams—our son's dream of his death before he was twelve and my dream of his death a few months before his birth—that also revealed their place in this living puzzle. Our son Pisti, the girl he loved, Jenny, my husband Istvan,* and I were later to discover that we were all participants in a reality that was far larger and more inclusive than we could have imagined before we entered into this most unusual journey.

I now perceive these extraordinary events not only as the mind's powerful response to death but also as a living design delicately woven into the larger web of the creativity of our time. These experiences are part of the new "wave of organization" that is moving through consciousness and transforming the worldview on our planet. At the deep levels of mind we are both the creators of and the participators in this wave of transformation.

Most of my adult life I kept a record of my dreams. When our son was very young, he told me his dreams and sometimes drew their images. As a young man, he kept his own journals. Had we not kept these records of our inner life, we would never have been aware of the relationship between the inner and outer events in our lives, nor could we have become conscious of their larger significance.

---

* Pronounced Peesh´ tee and Isht´ vahn. Both my husband and my son were named Istvan Kovács. Pisti is the familiar form of the name for the younger person. The English translation is Steven or Steve.

After our son's death, Istvan and I recorded our experiences on audiotape. We were aware from the beginning that our minds were opening to new dimensions of reality, and we wanted to map carefully and accurately our experiences of this reality. There were so many of these experiences that I spent more than three years transcribing them before I could begin the writing of this book. However, this turned out to be a valuable exercise, for it was during these years of transcribing that I began to experience deeper and deeper levels of the interconnectedness of each piece of the material. The work became an extended meditation in which my mind became increasingly more capable of realizing the power and vastness of this new reality.

While the mystical experience is outside both sensuous and conceptual forms of language, the narrative forms of dreams, visions, and myth revel in images, symbols and concepts to reveal their intention. It was particularly helpful that I had been trained in the various theories of symbolic, mythic language and that I had taught these theories in classes on mythology, the fairy tale, and other forms of symbolic literature for more than twenty-five years. I had worked with psychologists, and we had discussed our dreams on a daily basis for years. I was willing to apply to a symbolic structure any theory that would allow that structure to release its intention. I was also willing to forget about theory and simply allow the dream to live in me and reveal itself in its own way and in its own time.

Over the years of working with personal symbolic material I have become convinced that only the mind that experiences the dream or vision holds the actual key to its power, for that mind is connected to the feelings and experiences that gave birth to the symbols. While there can be great value in reflecting on the dream or vision with others, ultimately we need to trust the mind that perceived the symbols to "transform them into a world full of meaning and purpose."

Many of the dreams and visions that Istvan and I experienced repeated certain perceptions and concepts from different perspectives. Rather than narrate each of the individual experiences, for readability I sometimes have combined the various perspectives into one experience. Istvan and I were amazed that the dreams, visions, and outer physical events in our lives fit together like intricate pieces in a puzzle. Inner and outer realities flowed together to form a seamless picture of creativity that certainly included us but was far larger than our individual lives.

In the writing of this book I have not been concerned with proving anything but rather with the process of transformation and the quality of life that emerged out of the visions. This process often called for more courage than I actually had, but I knew how damaging it would be to reject my own experiences. The German poet Rainer Maria Rilke was very clear about the consequences of this kind of rejection:

> *In the end this is the only kind of courage that is required of us: the courage to face the strangest, the most mysterious, and the most inexplicable experiences that can meet us. That people in this sense have been cowardly has done infinite harm to life; the experiences that are called "visions," the whole so-called "world of spirit," death, all these things that are so closely related to us, have through our daily defensiveness been so completely eliminated from life that the senses with which we could have grasped them have atrophied.*[11]

I understood this cowardice: I had experienced its "infinite harm" in myself, my culture, my planet. Such behavior is rooted in an understandable fear of what we do not know and, therefore, cannot trust. And, unfortunately, in these most personal matters cultural institutions often intervene with prescribed truths that exclude our own inner experience. *This is a betrayal of the deepest spiritual impulse within us.* To avoid any possibility of further betrayal many people have forever closed the doors to spiritual realities. Yet both betrayal *and* closure bring "infinite harm to life."

In my own effort to do no further harm, I have attempted to narrate these extraordinary experiences with respect and honesty. These experiences were positive, inclusive, and so creative that they completely changed our worldview. Istvan and

I were opened to realities that nurtured within us a deep respect for all life and a commitment to work on the transformation taking place within us and on our planet.

Chapter One

"You are enduring what every parent dreads – the unexpected call, the jarring end of what you considered 'normal life' and the plunge into eternity – whatever that may prove to be."

– Margaret Marsh[1]

And indeed we did plunge into eternity—an eternity that proved to be conscious and loving, cosmic and personal, and infinitely creative. The experience felt stranger than anything we possibly could have imagined, and yet somehow it also felt familiar. With this shift in perception, everything changed. Nothing, absolutely nothing, would ever be the same again. We were parents here in time and space who were grieving the death of their only child, but we were also two people who were experiencing something so extraordinary that grief and awe, sorrow and joy were consistently intertwined in our daily lives.

My husband, Istvan, and I were home that Tuesday afternoon when "the unexpected call" was received from the Huntington Memorial Hospital in Pasadena, California. Pisti, our son, had been in an automobile accident on the 210 Freeway. As the social worker and I spoke, Pisti was in the Operating Room. "How serious is it?" I asked. "Very serious," she answered. "Is someone with you?" By then Istvan was in the room. He had heard my end of the conversation. As I quickly related the information I had just received, I was aware that I had never seen Istvan look as he did in that moment. Only later would he tell me how, as he listened to my words, he knew that Pisti would die.

Later we would put the pieces of the event together. Pisti had been doing some work for his uncle in La Cañada and was on his way home to study for an exam, pick up Jenny, the girl he loved, and go to school that evening. As he passed through the second tunnel to enter the freeway, a commercial truck was stalled in the fast lane. As he came out of the tunnel, he saw the truck too late to stop. There had been no emergency equipment on the vehicle, and the driver had abandoned the truck and jumped the wall of the freeway. By a wonderful "coincidence," as we say in Western culture, a paramedic ambulance was only a few minutes behind Pisti. The paramedics immediately placed him on a life support system and took him to the Trauma Center at Huntington Memorial Hospital, which was just a short distance from where the accident occurred. Of course, I don't know who the paramedics were, but I have thanked them many times in my heart, for it was this "coincidence" that gave us thirteen days to prepare ourselves to walk the path of death with Pisti.

I knew that Tuesday afternoon as I quickly jumped into my clothes that something very big had entered our lives. I did not believe then that Pisti would die, but I knew that we had all entered a new and very different playing field. Istvan drove to the hospital with one hand and held my hand with the other in a grip that was far stronger than he realized. We were silent, both of us trying to absorb what was happening and trying in our own ways to prepare for whatever it was that lay before us. I knew Jenny would soon be expecting Pisti to pick her up for school. I dreaded calling her, but once we arrived at the hospital, we did call her—and now she too knew that her life would never be the same.

As we waited in the Trauma Center for Pisti, who was still in the Operating Room, my mind began to slow down, almost to slow motion. I thought of death, how I had feared it as a child, feared losing my mother who carried so much of my heart energy. I feared this because she and so many women in her family had lost their mothers when they were very young. Later I had feared losing Istvan and then Pisti. How strange, I now thought, that it was only during the last two years that I had been able to trust the universe enough—how else could I describe it—to release that fear. I had not lost my mother to death when I was too young to escape without deep wounds. She had lived to be a healthy, vital seventy-seven when, just one year ago, she was killed instantly by a car as she crossed the street. She had always wanted to die quickly, so there was a kind of fierce beauty in her death, a grace and completeness.

I had accepted this death, but I deeply missed her mother energy. Now death had called us again—or at least the very real possibility of death. At this thought my mind dispersed. It could not yet allow itself to place Pisti and death together. Instead, I found my thoughts coagulating around more general views of death. I thought about its power to completely undo us. Even a confrontation with the possibility of it changes us radically for the rest of our lives. Is it because of this power that it seems to dominate us, and, if not us personally, then certainly our media? But, I wondered, what about those persons who apparently kill randomly without feeling? Are they not, in a reverse way, also dominated by death? Are they not caught in an addictive relationship with it? In fact, is not the very core of Western culture—and most of the planet—also caught in an addictive relationship with death? We both fear it and pursue it. Surely death is our ultimate absurdity.

But this absurdity is also a mystery. How can the beloved child or husband or wife or mother or father or brother or sister or friend be with us one moment and be absent the next, absent forever? How can this be? The simple response that life creates a unique form randomly and then abandons it just as randomly is not functional when we ourselves are confronted with the actual experience of the death of what we love most in the world. Many abstract theories tend to dissolve during real experience. Certainly, I knew, in this moment, they were dissolving in me. I was beginning to feel something vast moving in the deepest layers of my being. Strangely, I felt grounded, and I had a sense of some great mystery ever so faintly beginning to awaken in me, not in my head but in my body.

Suddenly, I realized that I was hardly breathing. I looked at my watch. We had been waiting only a few moments. The neurosurgeon was standing in the doorway. I heard her say Pisti's condition was very serious. His brain was pervasively bruised and swollen. He was on every machine in the Trauma Center. If he lived, he would not be the person we knew. "He is not in my care," she said. "He is now in God's care." I heard these words, but they remained outside a reality I was fiercely protecting.

Istvan and I were now allowed to be with Pisti. We looked at him in silence. Pisti had turned twenty just two months earlier. He was a tall six feet, two inches and had curly brown hair that had been shaved to allow easy access for the tube that was inserted into his brain, but it also allowed the strong, good-looking structure of his face and head to be more visible. I was deeply moved by his beauty as he lay there, unconscious, unmoving, and silent. Perhaps it was partly because this was a beauty so close to death that it no longer belonged to him alone but to that intense mythological moment when extreme forms of being hover in a delicate balance. Even his age, captured as he was between the boy and the man, gave him that "budlike capacity" of the mythological image to hold apparent "contradictions in perfect equilibrium."[2]

Pisti was our child, but he was also *the* child. I intuitively knew that as the knowledge of Pisti's accident spread quickly that evening, the response and the sorrow and the support would be not only for Istvan and me and the others who loved Pisti but for all children and for all families in the past, present, and future. One of the gifts of death that we were to experience was its power to weave all of us together into a conscious web of attention at the border of life and death where we would be forced to confront these ultimate mysteries of our existence.

I heard Istvan speaking to Pisti in a voice so deep in pain that it was hardly recognizable. I realized that he believed Pisti would die. Istvan was apologizing to Pisti for the time not spent with him, for the times he was more critical than helpful—and he was expressing his love for him. In so many crucial ways Istvan had been a very good father, but now, in the truth of death, he was walking in the full knowledge of all he could have been. Regardless of all we might actually have been, the power of death can bring an awareness of a much larger creative potential.

I was not where Istvan was because I did not think—or I did not accept—that Pisti would die. Yet, I heard myself whisper to Pisti that if he chose to live, he could return whole and well, but that if he did not choose to return, he must release his body to death so that he would not be trapped in matter. Finally, I said to him that if he chose to go, we would let him go. Where did these words come from? I had no intention of letting him go, and yet something in me was already preparing for that possibility.

I can't say that I really knew Jenny very well before Pisti's accident. She was very shy and quiet. He had been attracted to her for years before they actually started dating. In April of the year Pisti died they had gone to Mount Baldy together, made a Medicine Wheel in the earth, and, hand in hand, they had walked the positions from the South around to the East. They read poetry they had composed for the occasion to each of the four directions, and they asked the Great Spirit of each direction to bless their relationship. In this way they had committed themselves to each other. Now Jenny, Istvan and I were together, locked into the same destiny with this great mystery for which none of us had been prepared—or so we thought.

Istvan and I came to realize that this young woman, who was only nineteen years old, had great strength. We were often together twenty-four hours a day. At the very least, we were together from early in the morning until late each evening. Somehow the three of us rather quickly decided that we would try to live only in the moment and to walk the path between opposites. But what did this really mean on a day-to-day basis? It meant that we tried not to think in terms of life and death—these two huge, apparently opposing principles of existence. We simply tried to evaluate all the evidence of each moment. How was Pisti at this very moment? Was there anything we could do in this moment that would qualitatively add to his or our well-being? We struggled not to play the game of "what-if," but rather to imagine Pisti whole and well in spirit, completely free to follow his own path. Moment by moment, we tried to release ourselves to the choice of his soul, to remain unattached to the outcome but completely committed to the quality of his process—wherever that process might lead him. Of course, this struggle was like walking the razor's edge, and we often fell off, but one of us or our friends would pull us back onto the path.

Jenny was often the one to remind me that I was stepping outside the moment. I knew the incredible pain she must be experiencing. In Pisti she had found someone who understood her, loved her, respected her, and believed in her. She knew the possibilities that now lay before her, but somehow she also knew the most creative role for her was to stay on the path that allowed him the greatest freedom, even if it meant losing what she wanted most in life. The better each of us learned to walk this middle path without inner demands, the easier it was on us. There was evidently something in this approach that was consistent with the principle of life itself, so that even in our deepest pain, we felt an unexpected energy supporting us.

One day followed the next as we walked this difficult path as best we could. The world was not the same. Nothing even looked the same, and nothing felt the same, or smelled the same. However, the Trauma Center was relatively new and quite beautiful. Having been in dreary hospitals in other parts of the world, I was able to appreciate the soothing quality of this beauty. I also knew that Pisti was receiving the best care Western medicine could give him. We were allowed to be with him only a short time each hour, but, of course, we were always in the Trauma Center except for those evenings when there was nothing for us to do but go home and try to rest our minds and bodies. I was so exhausted on those evenings that I fell into a deep, dreamless sleep only to awaken each morning to the horror that was occurring in our lives.

In spite of this reality, there were gifts of the soul everywhere. The love, empathy, generosity, and genuine friendship of so many people mitigated our pain. People came every day, all day, and into the night bringing their gifts of the heart. Often they simply sat with us in silence as we tried to absorb the steady decline of Pisti's condition. They brought food, hot chocolate, coffee, and love. Sometimes they admitted they felt helpless, but I always tried to remind them that they were helping us carry the weight of this sorrow. This was something I learned on a deep level and continue to experience even today. I did not really know before Pisti's accident that friends can lighten the load of grief by feeling it themselves, by holding in their consciousness what another is suffering. This empowered us.

One evening the neurologist on duty told us that we might lose Pisti within the hour. There were three things that could be done—and they were being done even as he spoke—but there was very little chance Pisti would live. Istvan and I stood in the hallway alone. I don't know where Jenny went. The Trauma Center was filled with friends. Some were in the waiting room, some downstairs in the lobby, others outside on the patio. Istvan and I stood in silence and held hands.

For more than thirty years Istvan had balanced my life with his extraordinary optimism and his love for life. He had a way of looking at the world that seemed to dissolve anger, so he was not angry now, nor was I. There really is no word for what parents feel when they stand on the border between the life or the death of their child. Everything we had experienced since Pisti's accident was now curled tightly into the circle of an hour. I tried to hold the middle ground as before, but I felt an energy coming from Istvan that was so powerful that I quickly looked up at him. In his face I saw his enormous struggle to contain his sorrow. The intensity of his feeling was so strong that I feared the energy would explode. Would this extraordinarily healthy man have a heart attack? Where could this energy go? How could it be managed? I heard myself speaking words to him that now seem so simple, but they rolled out of a depth of conviction that must have been healing. "Istvan," I said, "if we are called on to do this, we can do it. We can do it." I don't know where my strength came from unless it was that we had been partners for so long that we had created a system of balances between us. For the rest of the hour we stood together in silence.

During this hour Istvan's feeling would reach such an intensity that his life would be qualitatively transformed. Later, when he was able to talk about it, he said that his love for Pisti and the acute pain he was experiencing as Pisti hovered between life and death totally filled every aspect of his being. Nothing else existed in the world during that hour. He explained how the tension reached what seemed like an unbearable degree, and then suddenly this energy exploded into images that played out their composition before his eyes. He saw Pisti sit up in bed, open his eyes, and reach out with one hand to catch a dove with a ball of fire, which he placed in his heart. Then he lay back down. The scene changed from the hospital room to Machu Picchu in Peru. Istvan "saw" Pisti standing on the small mountain to the left of Huayna Picchu. Pisti was looking up at the sky and holding his left hand up, as if to receive something from the heavens. His right hand was extended toward the earth, as if to give to the earth what he was receiving from above. Everything was calm and silent. Istvan was filled with a deep peace. Love flowed between Pisti and Istvan, and this love seemed to fill the entire world.

When Istvan described this experience to me, I was reminded of Ernst Cassirer's description of one of the ways symbolic language emerges into human consciousness. I had spent much of my life studying theories of consciousness, how the rational mind functions, and how dream, visionary, and mythic images form and function in the mind and in culture. Istvan had not spent his time thinking on these matters. While he was open to my interests, his had always been very different. So I was especially impressed now that Istvan's experience paralleled Cassirer's description. In his work on symbolic forms, Cassirer explains that when a person is "under the spell" of the organizing principle of the symbolic and mythic, "it is as though the whole world were simply annihilated"; the focus on a particular content is so complete that nothing else exists. On the one hand, the entire self is "possessed" by a single concern, while, on the other hand, there is an extreme tension between the self and the outer world. When this energy becomes overwhelming, the tension is released and bursts into the formation of the symbol, which then confronts its own mind in a drama of felt meaning.[3]

Istvan had no idea what these symbolic images *meant*, but he certainly knew what he felt. He did not know whether these images related to Pisti's living or dying or neither, but the experience had the effect of allowing Istvan to accept whatever came because he had the experience of the living presence of Pisti as a bridge between the worlds we call life and death. Within the experience itself, the words *life* and *death* would have been insignificant because, as Istvan explained, "I felt the whole universe was alive." And he *knew* that the love between Pisti and himself was indestructible.

Pisti did not die during that hour. We continued our vigil. Upon arrival at the hospital, Pisti had been given a medication that allowed his brain to rest completely for several days. During this time the machines did all the work for his brain. When the medication wore off, we expected him to give signs of life if there was any chance of survival. When the day came that all the medication should be out of his body, we were hopeful.

Early that morning I had a powerful dream of spirit beings running toward me, one after the other, each asking me quickly and distinctly, "Are you ready? Are you ready to accept this? A miracle, a miracle." I answered in my dream state, "Yes, yes, I'm ready. I am ready." When fully awake, I pondered this. I knew that the deep layers of the mind have a different mode of perception than the highly focused conscious mind. In this mode the mind can perceive the *intention* of the organizing—or dissolving—principles of life, both within its own individual form and within the larger web of life. This knowledge can then be released to the conscious mind in symbolic language, which is the language native to these deeper levels of the mind.

So I thought that this dream might—perhaps—mean that Pisti was going to live, to be miraculously healed. I told Jenny and Istvan. We talked about it on the way to the hospital. I knew, of course, that the mind that dreams and creates waking symbolic visions is the part of the mind that views life and death very differently from the part of ourselves that we refer to as *I*. So we were cautious. Could some part of myself be suggesting that Pisti's *death* would be as much a *miracle* as his life? We tried to stay open and balanced, but the dream had given us hope in spite of ourselves.

We arrived early at the hospital and anxiously went into Pisti's room. We were so disappointed to learn that not only had there been no sign of life from Pisti but he was worse. The pressure on his brain was continuing to increase. It was in that moment that Jenny knew, and the two opposing principles of hope and despair collided in her. As the three of us looked at Pisti and watched the numbers rise on the machine that monitored the brain pressure, my concentration was broken by a sound coming from Jenny that was not loud, but somehow I knew it signaled the collapse of hope, the beginning of a letting go that would take years. Istvan quickly caught Jenny in his arms and held her while she cried.

Still we waited. From the beginning we had made it clear that we did not want any attempt to keep Pisti alive artificially. We had agreed that Pisti would be removed from the machines once the doctor knew there was no hope. Finally, that day came. We had expected it earlier, but it was on Friday afternoon, November 8, that the doctor called us into the small conference room in the Trauma Center. The last tests showed no brain activity. We agreed that the machines be removed immediately. The official death process had begun.

I looked at my watch. It was a few minutes after four. It was on this very day at this exact time one year ago that my mother had been killed. This was another "coincidence," but a strange and deeply felt coincidence. In Western culture we don't know what to do with such occurrences. Usually we notice them and then relegate them to the "Strange Coincidence Department." A more rational and respectful approach would be to record all such experiences in detail and to wait and to observe—not with the prejudiced conviction that we are dealing with nonsense, but with the respect that all data deserve. Perhaps, if we have enough pieces, a larger picture will emerge.

During these days in the hospital, when our minds were tightly stretched by the tension between what we perceived as life and death, a larger picture did begin to emerge. Some of the pieces of this picture came from past experiences that we had not fully understood, but that we had recorded and saved. Now pieces were emerging almost daily. With Pisti's accident it was as though we had entered a highly charged energy field of strange coincidences, synchronistic events, powerful dreams, and waking visions. Experiences that had earlier appeared to be unrelated were beginning to reveal a poetic logic that was organizing these fragments into coherent form. The picture that was emerging included our own individual lives as integral narratives within a much larger pattern. Our "plunge into eternity" did indeed bring "a jarring end" to everything we had considered "normal." We were now open to a life force that was infinitely creative, yet we were painfully aware that this force included our experience of Pisti's death.

We left the conference room. Pisti's path was clear. We no longer had to walk the middle ground between possibilities. Death was now our reality. Except for the respirator, all the machines were removed from the room. The nurses who had given him such excellent care were also gone. Each of us took turns sitting in the room alone with Pisti—alone with the truth. I looked out on the flat roof and watched the birds play in the rain. I thought of the families or single parents who had no insurance. I thought of those who had to go through this experience without a partner or friends or community. I mourned for those who had received news of a sudden death or a violent death of their child. We had thirteen days gradually to become conscious of Pisti's leaving this world. I was grateful for the many things that helped me bear what seemed unbearable. I looked at Pisti. He still looked serene and beautiful. I laid my cheek on his hand. Now I could give myself to grief.

Chapter Two

"We are far more out of touch with even the nearest approaches of the infinite reaches of inner space than we now are with the reaches of outer space. We respect the voyager, the explorer, the climber, the space man. It makes far more sense to me as a valid project – indeed, as a desperately and urgently required project for our time – to explore the inner space and time of consciousness."

– R.D. Laing[1]

As I gradually became conscious of the outer conditions of the culture into which I was born, the emptiness I experienced was so intense that the only truly "valid project" of my life could be the exploration of "the infinite reaches of inner space." My earliest memory of the dark and confused side of the outer reaches of my world came one Sunday afternoon when my brother and I were listening to the Gene Autry show on the radio and heard a strange voice announce the bombing of Pearl Harbor. I was four, almost five, then. Our parents sent us out to play. It was later explained to us that the world was at war. But what did that mean? I kept asking my mother why adults were allowed to fight when my brother and I were not. My mother tried the best she could to explain why grownups went to war, but her explanations did not make much sense to me.

As I grew older, each Saturday afternoon at the movies I saw the news of killing and the destruction of what looked like whole worlds. I no longer asked adults about these serious matters. I had learned they did not understand either. I no longer even questioned them myself. I accepted that this was the way the world worked. I could not have given words to my feelings then, but I can still remember the pictures I saw on those Saturdays and the emptiness and confusion they caused. Little by little I was becoming aware that the world I had been born into was a world so ill that it would try in every conceivable way to destroy itself.

On a day-to-day level, however, I lived my child's life of school and play and chores, relatively unaware of the horrible threads of violence and despair that were weaving their tapestry in my mind. Consciously I could put the war aside since my only contact with it was through disconnected words and images. However, these words and images left an underlying disturbance that as yet had no adequate language. Often I would experience a deep need for something I could not name. My first response to this feeling was that I was thirsty, but I quickly discovered that water was not the answer. I don't remember mentioning this to anyone in my family, probably because I did not know how to put these feelings into words. It was only much later when I reached a degree of consciousness sufficient for me to think about my past that I could see how these threads of my culture had begun to stitch into my mind at such an early age its myth of meaninglessness, emptiness, violence, and death.

This, of course, was the myth experienced from the underneath side of the cultural tapestry. The top of the fabric had a different design: the message communicated to me from every major cultural source was that I had been born into the most advanced civilization the world had known. The Western world had achieved the apex of mental development. It was the first civilization to differentiate rational thought from the dreaming, feeling, intuitive mind. It was the separation of and severing from these *inferior* functions that had allowed the *superior* function of rationality to achieve the great advances in technology, medicine, industry, and abstract knowledge. In school I was trained how to use the rational mind, how to think logically, and I was equally trained to repress feeling because feelings were not to be trusted; they could distort the logic of one's conceptual thinking. Dreams were chaotic nonsense caused by overeating or the mind's need to flush itself out for a clean day of reasoning come morning. If the rational mind were deceived into thinking it observed *meaning* in a dream, it was only that the rational mind itself had *attributed* meaning to it. This was obvious since only the rational mind was capable of logical intention. There was no such thing as intuition. Waking visions were a symptom of madness.

At home there was far greater openness. Perhaps it was the Irish in my mother that kept her open to the mystery of being alive, to the reality of experience that could not be explained by the rational mind. With her I lived in the reality of feeling, the power of dreams, visions, and intuition. She told me the stories of her family—the early deaths, neglect, poverty, insensitivity, and lack of fulfillment. Yet in her the mystery still lived. For her, life was filled with possibility and hope. I loved her and my father—for all his aloofness—and my brother, and this love validated the reality of feeling. I knew that if I did not have this love, I would not want to live. I observed in the Saturday news at the movies that people did not appear to have this love, so a fear of losing my mother and being thrown out into a loveless, feelingless world dominated my childhood. Therefore, the feelings of love and fear were real in my world in spite of what I was taught in school.

It was inevitable that both sides of this cultural tapestry would live inside me—along with all that was denied. A part of me accepted the greatness of Western civilization and enjoyed its material benefits. Another part of me experienced the contradiction of this cultural myth, its gnarled and knotted undersided ugliness. And on a daily basis I experienced realities that I was taught had no reality. Although this painful contradiction could not yet consciously shape itself, it created an inner intensity to learn more about both sides of the fabric. Later, I would be driven to study the design of Western thought systems and to discover why the reverse side of the dominant system revealed such destruction and despair. Only then would I be able to focus consciously on the culturally excluded realities, and only then would I understand that this brutal and violent contradiction in my culture was the result of all that it had excluded. The very structure of Western historical consciousness was built on all that it had denied. I would also learn that our healing could only come from those *realities* we had denied, devalued, and excluded from our rigidly protected view of the world.

To explore these denied realities I had to step into "the inner space and time of consciousness." I could now see that this had been the deep intention of my mind since childhood, for within these "infinite reaches of inner space" was the mind's knowledge of how to heal itself. Since this illness was rooted in the culture itself, such an exploration was not only "a valid project" for me, but "a desperately and urgently required project for our time."

Before Pisti's accident, Istvan had respected and supported my "project," but he had not been interested in these matters himself. Pisti was different. Out of his own despair with the outer world as a teenager, he became very interested in "the inner space" of his own being. What I was to realize after Pisti's death, however, was just how deeply both of them had been involved in the same "valid project." The days and years that lay immediately ahead were to reveal this to me in startling and unexpected ways.

From the moment we received the telephone call from the hospital, Istvan had known that Pisti would die. During our vigil in the Trauma Center with Pisti, however, Istvan tried to allow hope to exist and to release the terrible knowledge he had about Pisti's death. Later he told me how he had known. Two weeks before Pisti's accident Istvan was working in his office at home when suddenly he "saw" Pisti's car beside a freeway. He knew Pisti had been in a terrible accident. Superimposed on the car was Pisti's body. Istvan said, "I knew Pisti was dead because his car and his body were in two different dimensions, one superimposed on the other." Then he heard Pisti say, "Dad, I will be out of the house for a little while." When Pisti spoke those words, Istvan felt a strange sense of acceptance. Istvan said, "I knew it was time for him to do this, for this event to take place." Then the vision was over. The suggestion alone of such an event was extremely painful, but that Istvan had accepted it as necessary was equally painful. Then, suddenly, he couldn't remember the vision or even that it had occurred—until the fateful telephone call from the hospital two weeks later.

Istvan and I thought about this event. Here was an example of the deep layers of the mind communicating with its own consciousness, not with the powerful intensity of the vision

Istvan had experienced in the hospital, but rather as a surprise visitor slipping through the door between the unknown and the known while consciousness was focused elsewhere. We had no idea what Istvan's acceptance of Pisti's death meant, but we did know now that the vision had correctly portrayed Pisti's accident and death. But why had Pisti said he would be out of the house for a little while? It just didn't make sense—at least not yet.

Then there was also the case of Pisti's own dream when he was almost twelve years old. One afternoon I was vacuuming the carpet in the living room when Pisti came in and told me he had just remembered a dream he had the night before. I stopped working, and we sat down so Pisti could tell me his dream. He said that it was an important dream and asked me to write it down for him, which I did. He also wrote parts of it in his own journal. He was so impressed by the dream that he drew a picture of it. Since my life "project" was to understand all functions of the mind, I always took time to hear Pisti's dreams, and I recorded my own almost all of the time. This dream was the most disturbing dream he ever told me:

I am in a hospital room with white tiles all around. The four walls are white. Everything is white, the tiles, sheets, plastic, everything except some chrome objects and glass. The room is in 3-D. The sink is in the upper left hand corner and the table is in the middle. At first I cannot see myself. I am floating in an intensive care waiting room. I am above the roof but there isn't any roof. At first all I can see is the room. Then I am up above looking down at my dead body lying on the operating table.

There is a space of darkness. Then the scene changes.

I am standing in a horseshoe arrangement with nine other boys. In the center of the almost complete circle of ten is a blazing, non-moving fire. The light is in our faces, but it does not leave the circle. There are four boys to my left and four boys to my right. I am the fifth and I am looking directly across the fire to the aura of a person who seems to be the missing link. Outside our circle in the darkness there are two tanks seven yards apart. They are shooting lasers at each other, but they never hit each other. Explosions hit everywhere but not within our circle. The explosions never disturb our unity. We are all waiting for the tenth one to come. We all know that the tenth one will be me, and that when I arrive I will be complete because ten is the number of completeness.[2]

I asked Pisti what he felt during the "space of darkness," but he did not want to say much about it. "Maybe a little lonely," he finally admitted. "What do you think it means, Mom?" Pisti asked. I was privately struggling against taking the dream literally. I asked Pisti questions about his feelings during the dream. I cannot remember his answers and, unfortunately, I did not record this part of our discussion. What I do remember is that we talked about how death in a dream is sometimes symbolic rather than literal and that maybe the dream reflected his impending transition from a child to a young man. But the descriptive detail of the hospital room disturbed me. I found it difficult to interpret the dream symbolically.

There were several things about the dream that were haunting: the darkness between the two major scenes, the light filling only the circle as though the light and the dark were symbolic of different dimensions. The dimension of darkness contained conflict and action, the result of the opposing principles that appear in time and space. The dimension of light was characterized by undisturbed unity. Although this was a beautiful and peaceful scene, it gave me concern, especially since Pisti had just observed his dead body in the hospital and was now waiting for himself to arrive and to be received into this apparently eternal circle.

Then there was the mystery of the number ten. I knew that in some symbolic systems ten is considered a number of completeness. (In the *Kabbalah* the number 10 is considered complete because all other numbers are formed from the basic numbers in the unit 10.) However, Pisti had no knowledge of such systems. Even if Pisti had heard, willy-nilly, that the number ten is symbolic of completeness, I still had to consider the way his dreaming mind had used the symbol. I knew that the organization of a dream reflected the poetic logic of the dream. Here the number ten reflected the organizing principle in the structure of a circle where there was completeness, unity, light, and peace. The number nine, on the other hand, reflected the organizing principle in the structure of a horseshoe that allowed a space in the circle. The horseshoe was a structure in the process of becoming a circle. Nine was associated with "the missing link," but ten filled the space and completed the circle.

As I thought about this dream, I was reminded of the time in the hospital after all the life support systems except the respirator had been removed. We thought Pisti's heart would slow down, that he would gradually move toward death, and that the respirator would then be removed. We stayed with him that evening and all the next day. Still his heart beat vigorously. During the day we talked with the nurse about removing the respirator. It was painful to see Pisti's body "being breathed" hour after hour. The nurse spoke to the neurosurgeon on duty that weekend about removing it, but he would not give his consent. The respirator could not be removed until the neurosurgeon in charge returned Monday morning.

This was Saturday, November 9. All day we painfully watched over Pisti's body. This was particularly difficult for Istvan. He spoke once again with the nurse. "Wasn't there," he pleaded, "anything that could be done?" She understood what we were experiencing and she gently said, "You know, sometimes there are reasons beyond our understanding why such things fall outside our control. There must be some reason why we have to wait." This was a sensitive way of saying that absolutely nothing could be done if the doctor refused to give his consent, but it also reflected her openness to a different perspective of reality. Her creative attitude released us from the rigidity of a single perspective and allowed us to accept what we could not change. Yet it seemed so unnecessary for Pisti and all of us who loved him to be caught in this "no man's" space between life and death.

Early the next day, Sunday, November 10, we were awakened by a telephone call from the hospital. I heard Pisti's nurse on the other end of the line: "This morning the doctor agreed to send Pisti down for another brain scan. He told me that the report on the last brain scan was too indefinite for him to sign, but he has just signed the new report. We can remove Pisti from the respirator anytime today that you wish." Now as I sat with Pisti's dream and drawing in front of me, I was moved by the function of the numbers nine and ten on the last two days of his life. There was nothing any of us could do to complete Pisti's life on the ninth, but on the tenth everything fell into place. Our vigil at the hospital was completed, and Pisti stepped into the circle of light.

I knew that the cultural belief in the singular reality of the material world required that I ignore these experiences, but I could not do that. It had taken a lifetime to know how damaged the mind becomes when it attempts to deny such realities. I was now fifty-four years old, I had spent my entire life wrestling with this culture's deadly contradiction, and I had some familiarity with *denied realities*. I had studied to the best of my ability the design of Western thought systems, along with prehistory, early spiritual traditions, and psychology. I had taught literature, mythology and symbolic language for over twenty years and had completed my Ph.D. four years prior to Pisti's death. I was not a specialist, but rather a comparativist who sought an overview.

In my doctoral dissertation I explored the historical causes of this cultural contradiction and the resulting illness. I studied the relationship between the dominant cultural view and an ancient and powerful tradition that was denied, devalued, and repressed throughout Western history, except for those extraordinarily creative periods when it reemerged in an attempt to integrate with the dominant view. Each time this occurred, it was devalued, denied, and suppressed before it could be integrated. I learned that my own personal struggle was a reflection in miniature of the struggle of the larger historical culture. The history of Western consciousness reflects the perennial attempt of these denied realities to be integrated into the Western mind.

Their continued brutal suppression had resulted in our mental fragmentation and in violence.

Once I had finished my Ph.D., I was painfully aware of how little I knew given what there is to know, but I was even more painfully aware that I was short on real spiritual experience—which is another way to say that I needed more experience in these denied realities. I vowed to do whatever was necessary to experience my own wholeness. I therefore spent the four years following my doctoral work and before Pisti's death in this intense effort. I went to Peru to work with indigenous cultures that still value the *nonrealities* of my own culture. This changed me and began my preparation for the deaths that were soon to come.

With the experiences surrounding Pisti's death, there was evidence of a larger reality that simply could not be pushed into the shrinking model of the world I had been conditioned to accept. I would not and could not repress this evidence. After I had stalked other realities for a lifetime, fragmented though I had been, now these realities sought me.

As I began to gather the pieces of this larger picture, I looked through my journal that covered the period just before Pisti's death. I read the notes of my trip to Chaco Canyon and Canyon de Chelley in August and September prior to Pisti's accident in October. I had gone with a small group of people to meditate in these sacred lands. I read the dream of August 25, 1991, in Chaco Canyon:

> *I am lying in bed with a mother and her baby. Suddenly there is a huge crash: the baby is thrown violently through the window and then thrown equally as violently back onto the bed. Physically the child survives, but I know that the psyche, the soul, of the child has been shattered. I look over my shoulder, and, in a knowing glance Istvan, who is standing behind me, acknowledges this terrible devastation.*
>
> *In the next scene I am with the child who is now a little boy. I am the grandmother. I become aware that the boy is confronted*

> *with some kind of problem for which he verbally proposes a violent solution. I scold the child for even thinking of such a solution. The child looks at me with eyes that penetrate my soul, and he asks me in an adult's voice: "How long will it take you to understand what we must become to survive in this world?"*

When I awoke, I felt physically and emotionally shattered. I felt a loss so deep and so pervasive that I sat in the tent that morning and wept uncontrollably. The child in the dream was both my child and the World Child who has inherited this horrible myth of violence that we have let loose on our planet. This inheritance was destroying the souls of our children. I had known this with my mind, but now I was experiencing its reality in the consciousness of my body.

I remembered telling Pisti this dream when I returned home, and it reminded him of a dream he had about a year earlier. He dreamed he was in his room painting on a large canvas. A great spirit appeared behind him, and Pisti asked the spirit what we can do to heal the earth. Suddenly, the spirit was in Pisti's right hand and was painting a woman holding a child in her left arm and looking back over her right shoulder at the coming storm. Pisti remarked that the dream was pretty straightforward since it was evident that the child needed to be protected from a very present danger. "But," Pisti added, "just in case I missed the point, the spirit said, 'Protect everything that is coming into being.'"

As we talked about ways adults can and cannot protect their children, I thought about how Istvan and I had tried both to protect Pisti and to prepare him for the world he would be thrust into as a young man. I mentioned this to Pisti, and he said, "Yes, I had a near perfect childhood, but still I was not prepared." I thought of him as a child, surrounded by loving adults and good teachers. He had been a happy, confident child. Then came the fateful years of puberty and high school. Istvan and I saw Pisti become less confident and more melancholy. The wit and happiness of his childhood disappeared. On a deep level something was missing. I knew he was looking for something he could not find.

I had recognized these symptoms all too well and had mourned the fact that the same underlying disturbance of my youth was beginning to manifest in Pisti's life. It seemed as though the power of this disturbance throughout our culture was becoming more intense with each generation. It was no secret to Pisti or to most of the young people who frequented our home that the world was profoundly out of balance. A few years earlier Pisti had painted a huge, out-of-balance yin-yang image erupting into a world holocaust on the wall of this very bedroom, which now looked peaceful and serene and where now we were having our conversation about protecting the young.

This was the last long conversation we had before his accident that was only a few weeks away. He had experienced the shattering effects of a culture that is so out of touch with the inner realm that, in Laing's words, "many people can now argue seriously that it does not exist."[3] During those perilous teenage years, like so many of our children, he had walked the border of emptiness and despair. And again, like so many of our children, he had wrestled with addiction. I knew very well that the children of a culture are the mirrors of that culture's strengths and weaknesses. The pervasive collapse of the psyche in our children at an increasingly younger age is an emergency call for all of us adults to enter into that most "desperately and urgently required project for our time"—the exploration of our own "inner space and time of consciousness." We can no longer pretend that such an exploration is only for those with strange interests. For even if we feel that we and our children have been spared the worst, neither our culture nor the planet has been spared.

Pisti's struggle did bring him through to balanced ground. His wit, joy, and confidence returned. He wanted to continue to work in art because it had been the artistic process that opened and kept open the gate to his own "inner space and time." It was this inner journey that offered meaning and balance. As we talked that afternoon about his struggle, he said he would like to be able to paint very well and "then," he explained, "when someone looks at my painting, I'd like to hear that person say, 'I could do that!'" He hoped in this way he could help young people through the difficult passage from childhood to adulthood. This would be his way of trying to "Protect everything that is coming into being."

I knew my own dream in Chaco Canyon reflected not only the deadly power of our material myth to shatter all that is coming into being but our culture's unwillingness to acknowledge this power. My own unwillingness was reflected in my surprised response to the child's potential violence in the dream. Perhaps we can only begin to understand the negative force in this myth when we realize that it is not so much a myth as it is the negation of myth. As has been observed by others, the material myth is what a culture falls into "at the very bottom of the barrel" when it has failed to create a myth out of its own inner experience. The material myth emerges by default when a culture does not explore "the inner space and time of consciousness." Such a culture becomes "so out of touch with this realm" that many people are able to "argue seriously that it does not exist." The argument of materialism is clear: there is no "inner realm"; such an idea is a fiction. How could it surprise me—or anyone—that such a view shatters the life spirit in ourselves and in our children.

This dream came two months before Pisti's death. I was stunned by the similarity of the violent action in the dream and in Pisti's accident: Pisti's body had been thrown through the window of the car, slammed into a truck, and then thrown back onto the seat, just as the child's body in the dream had been thrown through the window and back onto the bed. That morning in the tent I had mourned the spiritual shattering of all our children, and in the consciousness of my body, I had also mourned Pisti's impending death. Pisti had already walked through the shattering of the spirit. He had survived this perilous journey because his despair had led him "to explore the inner space and time of consciousness."

Chapter Three

"Listen to the force behind the force of pure creativity.
*It is the essence of Life."**

During the week between Pisti's death and his memorial service, I felt a need to look at the photographs of him that had been taken throughout his life. I spent several hours, starting with his baby pictures, then going through childhood to young adulthood. I remembered the slight sadness, but mainly the joy, I had felt as he lived through one form, left it behind, and took on a new one. I laughed as I remembered seeing him right after his birth and thinking, "My baby!" Even then there was something about him that seemed to communicate to me that he belonged to himself.

As I thought about just how hard he had to work toward achieving independence, I realized how much that struggle had taught us both. I knew that this long and natural process of parental letting go of the child and acknowledging the young adult was helping me now. If he had taught me to acknowledge his creativity and independence in life, surely I could remember this in death. But this meant accepting his death, not as an accident, but as his choice. Something in me felt that it was his choice, but I did not know. There was a part of me that felt confused and sad.

---

* Pisti attributed this quotation to Salvador Dali on one of his pen and ink drawings. I have not been able to find the source of the quotation, but the Dali Archives in Florida determined that it does not belong to Dali. It sounds like Henri Bergson, but I have no confirmation for this.

I went into Pisti's room, which had gone through its last transformation just weeks before his accident. He had removed everything from the walls, painted the entire room white, and hung only the beautiful and serene shamanic prints of Susan Boulet on the north wall. I thought of the many forms this room had been given by Pisti as he moved from one stage of consciousness to the next. Now it was calm and peaceful, a place for meditation. As I looked around the room, my mind was still filled with the photographs I had just seen—the many and changing forms of the person we called Pisti. Surely, there had been a coherent organizing principle that created each one of his many forms. Why, I wondered, would this principle cease creating just because it had dissolved its last material form? This was a reasonable question since the principle itself is not material but more like a "wave of organization."[1]

I knew the question was reasonable, but I did not have a *living* answer. As I thought about this principle of organization, I saw one of Pisti's portfolios leaning against the wall. I opened it and looked through his art work. One piece immediately caught my attention. It was a relatively simple pen and ink drawing: standing to the right of a self-portrait of Pisti was Salvador Dali. Between them was a quotation attributed to Dali that Pisti had addressed to himself: "Listen to the force behind the force of pure creativity. It is the essence of Life." In that moment I felt a living answer to my question. This was another deeply felt "coincidence." Had I found this drawing at any other time, it could not have had the powerful effect that it now had, coming as it did like an answer to my question.

I sat on the floor and thought about this quotation: the essence of life is the force behind the force of pure creativity. The speaker is saying that the energy that organizes the forms in the material world is not dependent on those forms, but rather it is dependent on its primary force, the essence of all life. Then I said out loud to myself so I could *hear* the answer to my question: "The energetic waves of organization and dissolution of material forms do not originate in those forms but in the formless essence of all life."

I knew that Pisti had been attracted to "Dali's" words because his own inner experience had convinced him that the source of everything in the universe is conscious and loving and that this consciousness creates a *force of organization* that can materialize in visible form. At death this force of organization completes its work in the material world and removes itself from its visible form, but continues to exist as a creative force.

Now that Pisti was dead, I was able to acknowledge that through our dreams and visions this *force,* or principle of organization in Pisti's life, had revealed to Pisti, Istvan, and me the coming dissolution of Pisti's material form. I decided that I would go through all my dream journals very carefully in an attempt to track down every trace of this creative principle at work in Pisti's life as it prepared to dissolve its form in matter. Maybe in these traces I would discover something of the essence of that principle not only in Pisti's life but in life itself.

As I tracked this dream and visionary evidence during the following months, the creative power of these images and feelings was so strong that, from time to time, I had to remove myself from the work. My mind and body were being pulled into a process of transformation. Only gradually would I realize that this process was necessary to realign the energies of my mind and body with my heart. Symbolically and literally, the heart revealed its position as the very nucleus of the life principle I so intensely sought to understand.

The first dream related to the theme of Pisti's life occurred in 1971 during my pregnancy with him. I had not recorded this dream, but I remembered it well. As I thought about it now, I was moved that, in this dream several months before Pisti's birth, I was given a visual presentation of the principles of creation and dissolution working in his life:

> *I am in the country. I enter a small building made of wood. I realize it is my mother's old school house. No one is there. I enter and go upstairs. It is twilight. Hanging from the ceiling are many Chinese lanterns. All are dark except one that is long and narrow, within which a beautiful glowing light is*

pulsating. I know that these lanterns are souls and that the one pulsating with light is the soul that will be born through me. It is not yet time for the others to be born. I see an old man sitting in a rocking chair to the left of the lanterns. He begins to smoke a pipe. The essence of the light in the lantern comes through his pipe, and the smoke creates a large framed painting.

I look at the painting and realize that it is a painting in action. I also realize that the painting is facing me so that I can contemplate it. The canvas is dark. Into the lower left corner of the painting I watch a young man enter. He is carrying a sack over his shoulder. I realize this sack symbolizes the work he will do in life. He comes to a gate that is called the gate of death from the young man's perspective and the gate of life from my perspective. He walks through it and continues a very short distance when suddenly he turns to his left. There are very high mountains that he quickly climbs. He makes a semicircle on the canvas as he then turns left again at the top of the left side of the canvas where he steps out of the framed picture.

As he steps out of the picture into space, there is a burst of multicolored lights. When he steps into this light, he dissolves into gold, then into pure white light. The painting is over. The old man rises and comes across the room to greet me. I am standing by a table of food. I invite him to eat, but he regretfully refuses as he gently touches my hand. He says he would so like to eat the food, but is unable to do so.

The dream was also a metaphor for "Dali's" statement. I knew in the dream that the pulsating white light in the Chinese lantern was flowing from the source of light, just as the child in my womb was flowing from the source of life. The old man was at once the light from the source and the individual creating soul who was drawing the light from that source into the womb/lantern. Through his "breath" he was co-creating in time and space the material form of the child who would be born through me. The source of all light, then, is the essence that is the force behind and within the old man. The old man, the individual creating soul, is the force behind and within Pisti. Pisti is his pure creativity.

The old man was announcing to me his arrival as a male who had a certain purpose in life that would not take him long to complete. Then he would return to the light. The old man, of course, continued to exist after the young man returned to the light. In his spirit form he could not eat of this dimension, but in "the inner space and time of consciousness" the two dimensions touched. I knew this spirit was not forcing his creation on me, but rather that we were creating together. As his mother in time and space, I knew there was a deep creative relationship between us.

I turned now to my dream journals. I had forgotten the following dream that was dated October 17, 1989, two years before Pisti's death:

I am walking down a dirt road in the country. I am with a young man who is evidently my son. On both sides of the road are booths that are like living monuments. There is a family in each one, the living members with their dead beloved. It is the moment of farewell. I and my son stop at one such monument and look at it. The beloved dead is a young man holding a letter apparently from his father. It seems that we are making a film. It is like a play within a play, and it seems to be the historical time of the Civil War. It becomes clear that the reading aloud of the letter by my son would be very effective in communicating the intention of the film. We also realize that we should enter from the back of the monument.

We do so. My son enters first. Then I realize that Pisti is my beloved dead. He can walk through the structure. This seems to be a very important message. He is dead, but alive. He has advantages of the spirit world, but he also has advantages of the physical world. As we enter the monument, the family and their dead son rise to greet us. It is a joyous meeting because we bring joyous news: the dead live.

The letter is not read. What is important is the news we bring. Evidently, we are the letter in action. There are many questions. My son answers them and, although I too am joyful that this great truth is indeed the truth, I am crying, or, rather, my body is crying. The pain and sadness from my own experience of the death of my son linger in my body even though I know he lives. I realize that this kind of suffering over death is a result of having lost all consciousness of the true nature of death. Even though I now "see" that "the dead live," the pain still exists in my body and causes it to cry.

Then the young man in the monument asks, "I've been concerned about my vision. I can't see. Will I regain my vision on the other side?" And my son answers, "Could you see while on the earth plane? If so, then you will see on the other side."

I wondered how I could have forgotten this dream, yet the dream itself reflected my resistance to the knowledge of Pisti's death. There was the initial displacement of just who was dead since my conscious mind would not let in the news that it was really my son. When I was able to "see" that my son was dead but that he was also "living," I was happy, but my body continued to cry. This was a correct reflection of the two ways I did react to Pisti's death. Part of me accepted it and was in awe of what Istvan and I were experiencing, but part of me continued to cry—and this crying seemed to originate in the body.

We were involved in making a film. Again, life was presented as a work of art. The historical time of the Civil War was especially significant. My God, I thought, my life had been a "civil war," a life-and-death battle within myself between the deeply-rooted cultural myth of empty materialism and a way of living that would nurture all life. The same is true of Western culture: the outwardly imposed myth of matter as the only reality wages a civil war against the deepest organizing principles at work in all of nature.

Just as in the dream before Pisti was born, the central theme of the film—and therefore of this dream—was that the dead live, that there are dimensions of reality other than the material dimension, and that these dimensions have an effect on each other. My son was dead, but he was speaking to the living and the dead. He was present, fully conscious, and able to answer questions with the knowledge of the spirit dimension. In this way he was able to affect both realms at once, and he was able to tell the young man that his ability to see on this plane would affect his ability to see on the other plane. In this situation my son was more than the form he had taken for earthly time and space. He was like the old man in the earlier dream.

Had I not just relived the powerful dream I had before Pisti's birth, my rational mind would have asked whether or not this dream could have presented Pisti as living after his death simply because my mind would not accept his death. Could this be another form of the displacement I had experienced in the beginning of the dream when I did not yet know—or accept—that my son was also dead? Was it wish fulfillment?

And my rational mind would have answered that there were three reasons why I could reject the possibilities of displacement and wish fulfillment: (1) since feeling is the key to significance or *truth* in the dreaming mind, just as logic is in the rational mind, I was impressed with the fact that the feeling in this dream was intense in its expression of both sorrow and joy; (2) there was a genuine sense of responsibility and happiness with the telling of this *truth* to both the dead and the living, and in fact, this *truth* was the theme of the film we were producing within the dream; and (3) the integrity of the entire dream rested on this central theme that not only do the dead live but life consists of at least two major dimensions that affect each other. This development of the theme exceeded what would be necessary for the displacement of an unacceptable truth.

Even without this rational evaluation, however, I knew that this dream two years before Pisti's death was profoundly connected to the dream before his birth. In both of these dreams Pisti—or his creating spirit in the form of the old man—was a bridge between the material and the nonmaterial dimensions. And this image of Pisti as the bridge between the two worlds was repeated in Istvan's vision when Pisti was dying in the hospital. In that vision Istvan experienced the living presence of Pisti as a bridge between the worlds of life and death. Was this recurring symbolism of the "bridge" an attempt to communicate something to Istvan and me that we still could not completely understand?

Was this an attempt of the principle of creativity, not only in Pisti's life but in all life, to communicate to us that it is possible and natural for these two dimensions to be connected?

As the pieces of this larger pattern began to fall into place, I was able to "see" the traces of what I had been calling the creative principle of Pisti's life—and life itself—and I was beginning to experience the living reality of this principle in ways that I could not have imagined in the past. Something was opening up in me—opening to a dimension so vast that I was stunned to realize how excruciatingly small a space I had been trained to live in and call reality.

The next significant dream was dated March 17, 1991:

I am in a small, private museum of Egyptian artifacts. I enter a small room. In the center of the room I see a figure sitting at a table. It is a living artifact—a black jackal. He is the size of a grown man, sitting with one leg crossed over the other, his face looking toward a window directly in front of him. He has a long, tapered nose, and his entire form is exquisitely shaped and highly polished. I contemplate him, and then I realize that he is in a deep state of meditation.

As I turn to my right and begin to look at some of the artifacts in cases, I suddenly become aware of the jackal figure standing to my right. He begins to explain the artifacts. He tells me that I can learn about Egyptology and the ancient world through books, but he can tell me everything. I don't need books. With this, I look at him and ask, "Who are you?" He then dissolves before my eyes. A panel of black wood appears in his place. Its very essence is a blackness that appears to be breathing. I realize that it is a living force. A voice answers me, "The All, the Void."

At the time of the dream I knew very little about Egyptian mythology. I wasn't even certain that there was a jackal figure. I had probably seen pictures of the jackal, and perhaps I had even read something about him. However, I had no conscious memory of having done so. Yet in this dream the exquisite form of the jackal burst full blown into my consciousness with such force that I could feel the living power of his presence during most of the following day.

He had offered me a way of knowing beyond books. He had offered to be my guide, and he had already shown me the nature of this other way: a deep state of meditation. But wait. He had shown me something else as well: his complete transformation before my very eyes. Did he mean that I too would have to go into the Void, the very source of life, and be totally transformed? This was disturbing. Later, when I had some time, I looked up the jackal in several books on Egyptian mythology. And there he was, the beautiful black dog, Anubis, "The Opener of the Way."

"The Opener of the Way"—but to what? All I knew was that he had demonstrated a "way" to the All, the Void, the source of all life. And this "way" was one of total transformation. Evidently, the jackal was himself a bridge between life and death, the material and the nonmaterial dimensions. In the dream he died to his jackal form in the material world and stepped into the nonmaterial All. He left me the sound of his voice and the image of creative darkness within the living wood. If he was to be my guide, I was in for a radical change. Now I really felt I needed to know more about his function in Egyptian mythology.

I could assume that the historical image of the jackal was not relevant to my personal dream, which was rich without this reference. However, the dreaming mind had selected a historical figure for its artistic composition, so I needed to take this fact seriously. I had spent a lifetime teaching students that there are no extraneous elements in an artistic composition, and that each element deserves our attention and respect. Why would I be less respectful of my own inner artist?

Therefore, I plunged into the historical material and discovered that Anubis was an integral part of the Egyptian rituals for the dead. Why, I wondered, would a dog be the chosen image for a crucial role in such rituals? I knew enough about the symbolic function in the human mind to know that this was an important question. The essence of the image was to be found in the image itself. So I had to ask myself what characteristics or behavioral patterns of the jackal allowed the Egyptians to associate him with death.

R.A. Schwaller de Lubicz had a deeper insight into the symbolic function of the jackal than anyone I read. Each animal in Egyptian mythology, he explained, could be used as a meditation to understand an essential function of nature. The jackal is a symbol of digestion, which is a destructive process. He tears the flesh of his prey into pieces, buries it, and digs it up to eat when it has decayed. These destructive processes are all associated with death. However, it is from the torn, decayed, digested food that the jackal is able to live: he transforms the *dead* matter into life. The complete process symbolizes death, not as an end, but as a transformation.[2]

So there it was! The jackal was not only a symbol of the bridge but of the necessary process we must undergo to create that bridge. He was a symbol of decomposition and radical transformation. In him these two principles could not be separated. He embodied "two forms of being ... carried to extremes" and exquisitely "balanced against one another."[3] It was this exquisite balance that made him "The Opener of the Way" to the All, the Void. Anubis was the Egyptian symbol of the force behind the force of pure creativity, the essence of life, not from the perspective of light, but from the perspective of darkness.

He had revealed that he was the essence, the force behind the force of pure creativity, when he said that he was the All, the Void, yet he had not presented himself as light but rather as darkness. He was both the essence and the path to that essence through death and transformation. I knew very well that this path of dissolution and decomposition, whether through death of the body or death in the "space and time of consciousness," was the missing link in my cultural mythology. Death and darkness were feared, denied, and repressed, yet the black god of death, Anubis, was the connecting link to light and life. He was the key to the circle of completeness, to continuity, to multidimensional awareness. I could not take it lightly that Anubis had appeared to me and offered to be my guide. Together we could bridge the missing link in the broken circle of my own personal and cultural mythology.

As I thought about this dream in light of Pisti's death, there was another obvious layer of meaning. Anubis, I learned, was traditionally the announcer of death.[4] He was Hermes, Mercurius, and the path itself that led the dead to the realm of light. Plutarch observed that the dog Anubis could see as well by night as by day. Thus, traditionally, he was black and gold, darkness and light.[5] Before Pisti's death, I thought of the jackal energy as beckoning me to die to my old self so that a larger perspective could come into being. Now I could see that this was, in fact, true, but it was also true that Anubis was announcing Pisti's death in the physical realm, for it was through Pisti's death that Anubis kept his promise to "open the way" to a knowledge beyond books.

It was clear to me that the way could only be opened if I were willing to walk the path of transformation. I shivered. What would this actually mean? I found it disconcerting that the substance that the jackal took into his body was poisonous for most animals, but for him it was life-giving.[6] I knew that with Pisti's death I had already eaten what had to be poisonous food for anyone who had ingested the myth of empty materialism. Could the jackal teach me how to transform this poisonous food of death into a life-giving substance?

On July 12, 1991, I had the first of two intruder dreams. The second one came the very next evening on July 13. The first one was like a nightmare:

> *A man jumps into the window of my bedroom. I know he has come to rape me. I am stricken with such terror that the rapist becomes concerned about me. He gently puts his hand on my hand and asks, "Betty, are you O.K.? Betty, are you O.K.?" In spite of his concern, I know he still intends to rape me. Then Istvan sits up in bed, and the rapist runs away.*

I was at Lake Tahoe for a few days with two friends when I had this dream. As I told them the dream the next morning, they stopped me when I said that the rapist spoke to me. One friend exclaimed, "Betty, I said that. I tried to wake you by shaking your hand and asking if you were O.K., but I couldn't wake you." Evidently, I had awakened them both in the night with deep sounds of groaning, but they could not wake me.

It is a well-known fact that when information is trying to break through the deep layers of the mind into consciousness, the resistance of the conscious mind may displace the material. If the resistance is especially strong, the information can take on the image of an intruder. A rapist is one of the strongest forms of the intruder image. When I awoke, I considered the possibility of a literal interpretation, that is, that the dream might be a precognition of an actual rape, but there was no feeling to support this interpretation. Rather, I felt a heavy sadness around my heart without the slightest knowledge of its cause. Therefore, I could only conclude, at least for now, that my conscious mind was in a state of resistance—to something.

The next intruder dream was not as frightening. I tried to figure out what I might be resisting, but with very little success. Then on July 30, I had the following dream:

> *It seems that I have just received news of Pisti's death, but then it is not news of Pisti's death but of my friend's son's death. Then I evidently forget that there has been a death at all, for someone has to tell me a second time that my friend's son is dead. When I hear the news this time, I seem to realize it fully, and I begin to cry. I cannot stop crying, for I am grieving on a very deep level. I see my friend, the mother whose son is dead. She is not crying. She looks serious, but she is very calm and peaceful. She has accepted the death of her son.*

As I read these dreams, it was obvious that my mind had been resisting the knowledge of Pisti's death. As the deep layers of mind attempted to communicate to my consciousness that Pisti was going to die, my conscious mind experienced it as an attempted rape. I wondered how I had forgotten this dream and especially how I had made absolutely no connection between this dream and the intruder dreams. Of course, I could see how not doing so had been a protection for me. Yet the knowledge of Pisti's death had existed on some level of my mind, but I was struggling very hard to keep it out of consciousness. In this dream the knowledge broke through, but the knowledge was immediately displaced onto someone else's son. I simply would not accept that it was my son, yet the dream told the truth. Even as my conscious mind rejected the knowledge, I mourned for the death of my own son on a feeling level.

This dream also reflected the two ways I did react to Pisti's death: I was both women in the dream, one who mourned and one who accepted. The fact that I both knew of and mourned Pisti's death on some level of my mind and body before he died probably helped me to accept his death when it actually did occur. But something else also seemed to be reflected in the image of the woman who could accept her son's death: was she perhaps a foreshadowing of what I might become as I walked the jackal path through the Great Mystery of death?

During August my mind left the theme of death for awhile and seemed to open up to an extraordinary form of energy. On August 21, I had the following dream:

> *A group of people are working with a woman to adjust her energy system so she is in alignment with the nonmaterial dimension. Then she and I enter a house. The adjusted person is to my right and to my left are many spirits sitting on couches and chairs. They are all men who are dressed in traditional business suits. One man is speaking in a foreign language. At first I wonder if he is an actor, but later I know he is not because his language is so difficult and precise that only a native could speak it. As the woman and I look at the male spirits, they realize we are afraid of them, so they immediately adjust themselves visually. Once we have no fear, we become aware that the entire house is full of souls from the nonmaterial dimension.*

I was very intrigued with this dream. Who were all these souls filling the house and speaking in a language I could not understand? While I was somewhat fearful of them, I did not experience them as intruders. Why had they come? Why were they sitting on the couches and chairs as if waiting for something or someone? Was some form of mental and emotional realignment taking place in me? Was this the jackal energy at work? That is, was the jackal a symbol for that "wave of organization" whose time had come to move through me and reorganize my entire system?

Four days later, on August 25, I had the dream in Chaco Canyon of the shattering of the World Child that had left me emotionally shattered.

Then in early September I had the following dream in which the expansive energy returned:

I am walking down the street with someone, and I look up at the sky in absolute amazement. A beautiful rose falls from the sky and lands at my feet. Then the entire sky opens up and another world reveals itself. I see beautiful fish flying in the sky and suddenly I remember that I had once been told that when you see fish flying in the sky, extraordinary things will begin to happen. Other wonders appear here and there in the sky. I celebrate the appearance of this other world.

Was this "other world" a reflection of the new organization taking place in me? Was I becoming the jackal bridge to another dimension? At the very least, I knew I was experiencing in these dreams the flow of energy between dissolution and organization.

On October 23 the themes of the dissolution of the old and the rebirth of the new occurred in the same dream. A terrible catastrophe had occurred on the earth:

I am sitting in the second or third row in a huge auditorium. Someone is on the stage organizing and giving directions. Evidently there has been a great disaster on the earth. Some people are seated and some are walking around. There is a need for someone to work with us all to heal "the raped heart." I stand without hesitation and begin to lead the ceremony to heal the raped heart. I have no fear that anyone will think I am intruding. I know exactly what must be done, and I respond to the need. People are open and grateful for the healing ceremony that everyone knows is a very sacred act. Slowly and carefully, we begin to dance the Round Dance.

I begin to speak out of a great universal center and my voice itself is healing. It is the voice of the Earth Spirit that flows through all life. People around the world hear and respond. I see an image of a television reporter who is calling in to report that he has picked up the message even at that very great distance. "We have it! We're with you!" he says. Then gradually people all over the earth begin to dance the Round Dance to heal the raped heart.

I pondered the meaning of the raped heart whose healing solution was to be found in dancing the circle. If, on some level, I had experienced the knowledge of Pisti's death as a rape, how was that part of me to be healed? How could anyone's experience of death be healed? But the rape of the heart symbolizes more than death. Rape is a violation of love, a violation of everything the heart symbolizes. How could these violations, which had exploded into a world catastrophe, ever be healed?

In the dream, the symbolic mind was communicating to me that not only could I be healed but the entire world could be healed. A planetary catastrophe had brought people together, and they were consciously working all over the globe. I responded immediately to the call for help. I neither questioned my knowing what to do nor worried about anyone else questioning me. I knew, and I acted on that knowledge. This allowed the life force to flow through me. All of us understood that our illness was the raped heart and that the ceremony was vital and sacred. The healing image was the circle, and the healing movement was dancing the circle.

Every system of thinking can be reflected in an image. Our Western thought system is symbolized by a straight line because we view life as having a beginning and an end. For us, life and death are opposites. We imagine ourselves walking the straight line from our beginnings in birth to the opposite end of that line where we meet our own personal end in death. For the Western mind, death is the great absurdity that rapes the heart. The dream, however, offers a different thought system—one that connects the living and dead ends of the straight line into a circle.

I thought about the imagery in Pisti's childhood dream in which the circle symbolized wholeness and completeness, and the horseshoe symbolized the "missing link," the space between the two ends. I wondered what kind of energy would be necessary even to bring the two ends of the straight line into the shape of a horseshoe, much less to connect them to create a circle. In Pisti's dream there had been a dark space during which he had felt "lonely" just before the formation of the circle. I knew that the dark space was the place of transformation, which always had to include a death of the old and a birth of the new.

Then I remembered the jackal. For some reason, I was startled to remember that the jackal was the symbol of this missing link. He was the key to transforming the straight line into a circle. Finally, I was able to put it all together: the jackal is a symbol of that innate knowledge of how to create the bridge between death and birth, whether that death is in the outer realm of matter or the inner realm of mind. Something deep in me had called this wisdom into consciousness just months before Pisti's death and, as I was soon to learn, I was not alone.

In my dream of the Round Dance people all over the world knew how to dance this circle. Only the deep layers of the mind could give us this wisdom. The *institutionalized knowledge* of Western culture could not choreograph this dance because it was institutionalized knowledge in the first place that had flattened the circle into a straight line by denying the validity of individual experience. What was missing had to be discovered by the individual. Each of us could learn to dance the space of the missing link only through our own personal experience of whatever was missing from the institutionalized knowledge of our culture.

The circle had not always been broken. Many cultures in the past and a few in the present, danced, and still dance, the circular, spiral dance as the most sacred of all rituals. The evidence from these cultures tells us that the outer dance both symbolizes and focuses the inner movement of consciousness as it spirals down into the depths of our own individual being. At the center of our deepest selves, we confront the divine, the cosmic Mind, the All—not as Other, but as Self. In the great ecstasy of surprise and love, we remember who we are. We know, as Gandhi knew, that "Birth and death are not two different states, but they are different aspects of the same state." There is nothing but life, and, in the words of the Classical scholar, Carl Kerényi, we are "the nucleus of the nucleus" of that life.[7]

Over the centuries Western culture lost or destroyed the ancient techniques of exploring this "inner space and time of consciousness." With this loss, the circle was broken and we fell into a straight line and the violent myth of empty materialism. This profound loss has resulted in a worldwide catastrophe: the heart of the world has been raped.

As I thought about people all over the earth dancing the sacred circle as we were dancing it in the dream, I felt that the earth was dreaming a dream to heal herself, that she was responding to her crisis with a balancing movement to bridge this missing link and to become whole. I was dreaming a dream to heal myself and to live on a planet that was also healed. I vowed to hold in my mind the image of this beautiful earth and people all around the globe dreaming together the sacred steps of the Round Dance.

The next entry in my journal is on October 28, the night before Pisti's accident. It is the last entry during his life:

> *I am in a forest in a beautiful, two-room, two-story wood and glass building. I am upstairs above a meditation room. The walls in the room below and in this room above are made of glass from the middle of the walls to the ceiling so that I am surrounded with the lush green of nature. I have just returned from meditating in the room below. It is twilight. I can see very*

well in the cool bluish, comfortable light that fills the room. I am taking care of a baby.

Then I realize that a great male spirit is sitting on the couch waiting for me. I am not at all afraid when I see him. Even though I don't recall ever seeing him in this form, we know and love each other. It is love that brings him here this evening—but there is more. There is a deep, inner purpose that brings us together. He is waiting for me to put the baby to bed. When I have done this, I sit on the floor next to the couch where he is sitting. We are entering into a partnership for some kind of work for ourselves, the child, and the earth.

I read my comment following the dream: "This soul was from the Hermes Trismegistus field of consciousness." One evening about two years before Pisti's death, I had a powerful waking vision. I had been worried about Pisti, and I think it was probably this intense concern that opened my mind to deeper layers of its own knowing. I experienced Pisti and Istvan as being the same creating soul, and I knew that this soul created out of the Hermes Trismegistus energy field—whatever that meant! I had read about Hermes Trismegistus, but I knew very little about this figure. In the years ahead, this was certainly to change.

I would not understand the Trismegistus piece of this puzzle until later. For now, however, I was impressed that the dreaming mind had informed me that I was beginning a project with a soul in another dimension. It was significant to me that the project included a child. I thought of the shattered child in the Chaco Canyon dream, and of how the day after the arrival of this spirit in my last dream before Pisti's accident, Pisti's body would also be shattered.

I thought of Pisti's own dream in which he asked what we can do to heal the earth, and a spirit painted through him the image of a woman protecting a child. It was also significant that a man whose appearance was unfamiliar to me and who was sitting in my living room without my prior knowledge did not even surprise me. In no way did I feel he was an *intruder*. Had my mind experienced a shift in perspective? Had some realignment of my consciousness with the deeper layers of mind actually taken place? It appeared that it might be so.

Before Pisti's memorial service, Istvan and I, Jenny, and Pisti's friend Woody were going through poems Pisti had written. Suddenly Jenny handed me a sheet of paper and said, "Betty, read this." As I read the dream Pisti had recorded on this sheet of paper, I remembered that he had told it to me one morning while I was quickly making us each a cappuccino. The dream was not dated, but I remembered that it occurred within the last few months. That morning I had said to him that it was a rather complicated dream and that he should be sure to write it down so we could talk about it later. I never thought of the dream again, but now I saw that he had recorded it:

> *I dreamt that I was sitting on a large couch in a strange cozy house lit by candlelight. My mother came in and sat down. We both fell asleep. I began to see hundreds of small white lit candles. I began to chant in a slightly higher voice and I had quite a powerful chorus. I shot out of my body and landed on the front lawn. Instantly I heard my mother grunt, "Come here" in a severely low voice. I raced in through the doors and walls without touching them, replying, "What?" (I can still hear and feel my chanting.) I saw an empty bed and couch except for my sleeping mother. I then awoke and carefully walked out so I would not wake her. Later I went back inside to join my awakened mother. "Did you hear my chanting?" "Yes," she answered, "it was very clear. Everyone in the house heard your chanting in their sleep." Then, "You are truly afraid, aren't you?" "No," I answered, "not really." I then crawled into bed and she left the room.*
>
> *Suddenly and quite quickly I got a very strong tingle around my body and saw a blinding white light surrounding my body. The touch of the edge of the blanket against my shoulders was very irritating so I pulled the covers over my head. I could see and feel the light through the covers fighting to get in. "I'm not a chicken!" I said, as I stopped resisting it, and gave in to it. I could see the fabric strip away before my face as the light forced*

its way in and sucked me up. I shot straight up out of the house and out of the atmosphere at such an incredible speed that I did not even have a chance to see the street lights as I rose above the city. I flew away from the earth and then whipped past the sun, continuously gaining speed. I melted past worlds and suns at a speed so intense that I felt them "pop" as they approached, then vanished, and I could hear the gentle wisp as they belted away all around me.

I landed once again on the front lawn and heard the same grunt of "Come here" and my "What?" response. But this time my mother's voice was louder, quicker, and desperate sounding. I came inside and saw my mother by the side of my bed with me in it. "He's not in good shape. You have to come back for him," she said, as I observed my behavior in bed. I looked like a drooling idiot. I couldn't handle the entire experience in one swallow. "I will. I'll be right here," I said, as I stumbled out the door.

I had to fly again, no problem. I began to doubt myself as I leaped from the ground to the roof. I looked up through the trees and saw a small group of birds flying. "If they can fly, so can I," I said, as I climbed to the second story. "I seem to be having some trouble flying," I said to my mother as I could sense the choppy, erratic breathing of my sleeping self. I jumped in the air and coasted for a few, then coasted downward and pelted myself against the roof of the underlying carport, releasing my final abrupt breath.

I then saw a hospital room where two people were scurrying above a blue patient's gown in which the wearer was reduced to sticky white paint. One figure was desperately trying to revive the puddle. All the while he was talking feverishly with a voice from "the other side" which was attempting to persuade him that the patient was reduced to a vegetable permanently. The figure said to the gown's puddle, "Come on, old lady, you can do it." It then occurred to me that this puddle was not me. I tried to open my sleeping eyes but I was still deeply caught. I then jerked up in bed – reality – and had to stare around me to get a grip.

That morning when Pisti told me this dream, nothing seemed clear. Yet, when he said he realized that he was not the puddle, I had said, "Oh, thank God. It was not you!" Now, of course, it was obvious that he realized he was not the shattered body because his consciousness had already removed itself from that body. It was absolutely remarkable to me that Pisti had left this record of his experience of his dissolution in matter.

I felt a strange sensation when I read that Pisti was sitting on a couch and that I came in and sat down too – just as had occurred with the spirit in my last dream the night before Pisti's accident. Then, after I left the room, Pisti experienced his dissolution in matter and transformation into light. I remembered how Pisti had stepped into the white light in my dream before his birth and how he had experienced his arrival into the circle of light in his dream as a child. In his early dream he had experienced a space of loneliness before his arrival into the light, and now, in this dream, he struggled against fear as "the light forced its way in and sucked" him up and out of his body and out of this dimension. The loneliness, darkness, and fear are a natural response to the dissolution of the body when experienced from the perspective of matter. It took Pisti some time to switch perspectives and realize "that this puddle was not me." His body was destroyed, but his consciousness continued to exist.

I found it incredible that in this dream he experienced what I would later say to him in the hospital: "If you do not choose to live, don't get trapped in matter. Come back for the body." He was aware in this dream that he had suffered a powerful impact that left him brain dead. And he knew that all of us – Istvan, Pisti, and I – knew of his death on some level of our minds before his accident. His soul had prepared all three of us for his return to the light, and as the time approached for him to dissolve his material form, we all were able to hear "his chanting" in our sleep.

I was deeply affected by the image of "hundreds of small white lit candles" and the sound of Pisti chanting in a "slightly higher voice" accompanied by "quite a powerful chorus." We had heard this chanting on some level that was not yet conscious. I was soon to hear this chorus again and realize the power and significance of its resonance. But for the present, I was very much aware that these were profound symbols of the principle of creativity in Pisti's life as it engaged in the process of dissolution.

Istvan, Pisti, and I had listened to and experienced—at least to some degree—the force behind the force of pure creativity. Sometimes it had been too powerful for us and we had displaced it or forgotten it. Yet this had been necessary for us to be able to live our lives together without fear. We needed both to know and not to know. Now Pisti was dead, and I was in a position not only to know but to place the pieces of this puzzle together. The creative principle working in Pisti's life had indeed allowed me to discover something about the essence of his life, and it also had allowed me to discover something about the essence of life itself. As I reexperienced each piece of this huge puzzle and then experienced for the first time the far larger reality that emerged out of these united pieces, I knew that the shattering of the myth of materialism in me was underway—and absolutely nothing could stop this process now.

Chapter Four

"Dad, there is nothing but Life."

"Our brothers and sisters on the earth are dreaming a terrible dream."

The conscious experience of this new reality with its power to shatter the old myth of materialism did not occur immediately after Pisti's death. This would take time. During the weeks and months following Pisti's death, Istvan and I were struggling to deal with Pisti's absence on a day-to-day basis, to return to work, and to create a new balance in our lives. I knew that Istvan, Pisti, and I had experienced strange visions, synchronistic events, and precognitive dreams, but I did not yet know the full power of these experiences. It would not be until later that I would have the time to study my journals. Yet Istvan and I knew we were walking in a highly charged field of energy in which these unusual experiences could only appear as random from a limited perspective. We felt that these events formed a precisely ordered sequence of connecting points in a web of consciousness too large for our present vision to perceive other than on a feeling and intuitive level.

The day following Pisti's memorial service Istvan and I were home alone, our responsibilities finally completed. As we stood in the kitchen that morning, Istvan mentioned that since Pisti's accident he had been having increasingly severe pains in his heart, as well as some difficulty breathing. He knew that the pain was from Pisti's death, but he said he was beginning to wonder if such pain could actually cause a heart attack. I was troubled. Like so many men, Istvan seldom mentioned pain in the present tense. It was Sunday, and he flatly refused to go to the hospital. In our despair we lay down together and held each other in silence. The tension created in my mind between the loss of Pisti and the fear of losing Istvan must surely have reached its maximum potential.

I don't know how much time had passed when I heard Istvan say, "Pisti was here." Both of us had experienced Pisti's presence. Istvan's pain was completely gone, and to our surprise and delight, it never did return. The former tension in my mind had relaxed into a calm ocean. For awhile we just lay there together unable or not yet willing to try to squeeze the vastness of our experiences into the tiny word forms available to us. Now we both understood what Pisti had meant when he said to Istvan in the vision, "Dad, I will be out of the house for a little while."

Finally Istvan sat up on the side of the bed and said, "I had no idea what you were talking about earlier. None. I will never look at the earth in the same way again." And he never did. Istvan had been radically changed. I thought now of this man whom I had loved since my twenties, how he had helped me survive the terrible emptiness I had felt in the world, how he had helped me live with greater ease and optimism, how he had respected my efforts "to explore the inner space and time of consciousness"—but how he himself had not had any interest in this effort. I recalled trying to tell him about a vision I had experienced a year before Pisti's death. At some point in my explanation I realized that he was not interested. When I asked him why he had no interest, he said, "I know you are telling me something that is important to you, but I have never experienced anything even remotely similar to what you are talking about, and I just can't relate to it." As Istvan returned to his newspaper that morning, neither he nor I could possibly have imagined what we were now about to tell each other.

"There is no way," Istvan said,

> *that I can even begin to put in words what really happened. I wasn't even here. I shot out of my body and flew through the universe at an enormous speed. I was inside what felt like a huge funnel, and as I was flying toward the central point of it, I saw thousands of images speeding past me: many places, some familiar, most unfamiliar, and hundreds of people from*

all races. Many of the faces were mine, some were Pisti's, and the others were a combination of us both. I knew, as if I had always known, how Pisti and I create together – sometimes as one person and sometimes as two people – like twins.

Things began to slow down, the images disappeared, and what had been the receding central point became a small circle of bright light. Gradually the circle became larger as it moved toward me. Then, slowly, the light formed into an image. When the image was clear, all movement stopped. There was complete silence. I could see that the image was Pisti sitting in a yoga position of meditation with his head bowed in a reverence so deep that it penetrated my whole body. In one hand he held the earth. I looked at it.

At this point Istvan broke down.

When he could continue, he explained that the earth had a large ring of pollution around it. Istvan didn't just see this; he experienced it. His consciousness moved into the pollution. The moment he entered, he became aware of the pain in his heart, and it began to intensify. He felt separated from Pisti, the light, and the deep reverence he had just experienced. There was only a terrible aloneness, emptiness and fear. He experienced the constriction and thwarting of all life forms as they struggled to survive in this atmosphere. Then he realized that this pollution was a result of the feeling of separation he had just experienced.

Suddenly he was no longer in the earth's atmosphere. He was once again consciously in the light, with Pisti, and permeated with a deep sense of the sacredness and interconnectedness of all life. He was in a state of joy, and he felt Pisti say, "Dad, one person could heal the earth if that person would love enough."

"I realized," Istvan said, "that love is the key to everything."

Pisti explained how respect allows us to be more conscious of love, but I have to say that I never experienced respect like I did today. It has a completely new meaning for me. I respected myself and everyone and everything else to such a degree that the whole world was sacred.

Once I felt this, the scene changed. Pisti's consciousness and mine merged, and we were experiencing our lives together as one person. I was Pisti and he was me. I felt like I was talking to a mirror image, yet the image was not doing what I was doing. Questions were asked and answered, I to him, to me, he to me, to himself. We were in some ways indistinguishable. During those moments I knew and understood everything that was happening around me. Then we were two people again, and I experienced our separate, individual lives. Pisti was by my side. We laughed and talked, and he explained our lives to me – why we are sometimes one, and sometimes two.

Together we looked down at my body lying on the bed. I was in the position of the black panther that was tattooed on his left arm – a crawling position with the right hand up and the left hand lowered. Then I reexperienced the vision I had in the hospital of Pisti standing on the small mountain next to Huayna Picchu. Pisti said, "It's a great symbol, isn't it! I reach up with my left hand and the essence of the other dimension flows through my right hand to your right hand and out through your left. We fit, and in this way we create a conscious bridge between the dimensions."

Everything Pisti said felt like a memory. I began to remember why we had come to the earth, why we were born. I knew that souls from all over the universe were here because of the critical state of the earth and its atmosphere. Pisti said that the next twenty years will be crucial years for the earth. Then the question came up of why I hadn't had any interest in these matters earlier. Pisti laughed and said, "You had to put that part of yourself on ice so that I could be born. If you had developed those aspects of yourself, the two of you might not have been able to conceive me."

Then I became aware of a feminine presence, and I realized that she had always been with us. She was as pervasive as air or breath. She had no face, yet she was the most beautiful woman. She talked about the earth and how it would be healed. She told me her name was Sira, and I knew, without her saying it, that she was pure love and creativity. Then Pisti said, "Yes, we are Sira. In the time-space dimension we are her masculine aspect. We create out of the Hermes Trismegistus energy field, and that energy is Sira." Then Pisti said, "Ask your mother about this. She will understand." When he said, "mother," I knew he meant you. With that, he and I began to remember our lives together again, partly, it seemed, as an explanation of why he had referred to you as my mother.

I saw several circular formations, like plates, just hanging in the air. As they became clearer, I saw you and me dancing on each plate. Each dance was slightly different. Pisti then said, "In other, parallel worlds, we are doing similar work. Sometimes you are the one who dies and I stay. The circumstances of each situation determine who stays, but in each world, you and I create a conscious bridge between these dimensions. The only one who always stays is Mother."

I stopped Istvan. "What do you think he meant by that?" Istvan answered, "I don't know exactly. I think he just meant that one of us dies in each realm, but not you. Pisti said that you would not be destroyed by death because you understand." Then Istvan told me that when he heard Pisti say this, he remembered that Pisti had died. "But death," he said, "didn't mean the same thing anymore." As Istvan started thinking about death and how much fear and suffering it brings on the earth, he felt Pisti say, "Birth and death are events in time and space." Then Pisti showed Istvan a circle of light. As Istvan looked at this, his mind felt intensified far beyond anything he had ever experienced. There was no end and no beginning. Istvan heard Pisti say, "Dad, there is nothing *but* Life."

Then Istvan remembered the dream Pisti had as a child and how he had stepped into the circle of light. "Yes," Pisti said, "I completed the tenth." I asked Istvan if Pisti explained what completing the tenth meant, and Istvan said, "He took his place."

"But," I insisted, "what does taking his place mean?" And Istvan responded, "He took his place." I desperately wanted to know more, but, at this point, I realized that Istvan was struggling with the intensity of an experience that simply could not be reduced to language. We both remained silent for awhile. Then Istvan continued,

> *Together we went to several of the sacred places of the world, Machu Picchu and Giza, and two other very ancient civilizations, which Pisti explained were no longer in the earth dimension. I knew we had deep connections to all these places, and it seems that Pisti talked about them, but now I can't remember what he said. Then Pisti and I were back here. I was once again lying on the bed, and he was sitting by me, holding my hand. I felt so much love and peace. Suddenly Pisti began to laugh, and so did I. Then he said, "You see, you old fart, we finally had a good conversation." Then I realized I was here by you.*

As Istvan and I sat on the bed that afternoon and told each other our experiences with Pisti, we were in a completely different kind of space and time. Istvan was able to maintain his conscious position in this new dimension. I was not. Yet I was the one who had always been interested in the possible existence of such realms, and I was the one who had studied other people's experiences through mythology, history, mysticism, and shamanism. I had even begun to have extraordinary experiences before Pisti's death, but now I was the one who had difficulty holding onto the vastness of what we were experiencing.

Istvan became my anchor in this new world. It helped me that he had previously read nothing about this sort of thing. When he entered the "space and time of consciousness," he did so with no preconceived notions. He was a businessman who had totally immersed himself in the outer world. In the early years of our marriage I had regretted his lack of interest, but I had accepted it because his love and independence, his strength and optimism had given me the stability that allowed me to explore the extraordinary.

Yet my exploration had rooted itself all too long in the academic world where the rational mind had been conditioned to believe in the fiction of its superiority over all other mental functions. I had not consciously accepted this, but the programmed response of this fiction was present nonetheless. Any participation in the *excluded realities* brought me up against a response of denial and distrust. The deeper I stepped into "the infinite reaches of inner space," the greater the demand and pressure I placed on my rational mind. I was asking my rational mind to allow information that did not support its fiction to coexist with that very fiction whose trained response was to deny and destroy it. In short, the more I experienced that contradicted the rational mind's structure of reality, the more vigorously it denied the validity of the experience.

So I too had a profound experience that day, but much of it was quite different from Istvan's. As I lay on the bed thinking about the pain in Istvan's heart, I, myself, started feeling very uncomfortable, and gradually I became aware of pain throughout my body. Then the pain centered around my own heart. A pervasive sadness moved through me and over me like an ocean that would surely drown me. I knew this sadness came from my fear that the universe was, after all, exactly what I had been taught—empty—EMPTY— of love and consciousness. Life was nothing more than a fluke. I doubted everything meaningful that had ever occurred in my life. I fell all the way down to the hard bottom of the barrel of materialism. The pain in my heart increased. I felt myself curl up in a horrible spasm of despair.

Then I felt a voice say, "Just stay with it. Let yourself experience it completely. Stay with it. You are at the very core of the myth of the earth." I was consumed by doubt. I felt restless, unfocused, irritable, fragmented—shattered. I lay there like an explosive ready to go off. Here at the bottom of the barrel—the core of materialism—there is no glue for the shattered parts.

The voice returned: "Doubt is, after all, not entirely destructive. It is not outright rejection without examination." That's true, I thought. One has to be open to have doubt, so I allowed my mind to go deep inside this doubt, and there I found my rational self armed to the hilt. It was determined to reject anything it suspected was less than the truth. Above all, it did not want to be betrayed. How could I not love this effort? But how could my rational mind move beyond doubt to acceptance of what the rest of my mind knew to be true? I had participated—at least on occasion—in the Great Mystery, but, simultaneously, my rational mind had participated in the denial of its reality.

I lay there stretched between despair and longing. I don't know how much time had passed when I began to hear what sounded like Native American chanting. It was powerful and haunting and seemed to be coming from a great distance. As the sound approached, the atmosphere became charged. I was no longer in ordinary space and time.

My consciousness moved out into space just beyond the earth. As I looked into the beautiful night sky, I felt Pisti's presence in the form of light by my right side. He and I moved closer to the earth, and I saw a large river of souls flowing like the Milky Way out of the vastness of space. The resonance of their chanting seemed to shape their circular movement into a great spiral that covered the globe as these souls were born on the earth. I knew that they would take in the poisonous myth of the earth and that their work would be to transform this dead food into a living substance. They appeared to be indigenous people, which I understood was symbolic of their harmony with the creative principles of life. They had come from all over the universe out of their love for the earth. This was a perfectly natural response of a loving universe to the pain and illness of our planet. I felt them say, "Our brothers and sisters on the earth are dreaming a terrible dream."

How well I knew this terrible dream, but I also knew that I was in the process of waking up. Pisti was chanting with this great chorus, and every cell in my body began to resonate with its deep tones. This was the same "powerful chorus" that had accompanied Pisti's chanting when he dissolved his form in matter. Earlier I could only hear this chanting in my sleep. Now I was awake and full of memory as we floated and spiraled in the great Milky Way of love and ecstasy. In this timeless moment we were in harmony with the deepest principles of the universe, and we were dreaming the dream of the earth to heal herself.

All of us—every single person—who had ever longed for a world of love and peace had called these souls to ourselves. Our deepest aspirations had created the field of energy necessary for them to be born on the earth. This longing is the thread that connects us to our deepest nature. How could it possibly be otherwise? How could we long for something from the deepest layers of our being that would be contrary to our own nature? Now, out of this very longing, we were creating new worlds.

As I participated in the mystery of this great river of creativity, I felt Pisti say, "Love heals the shattered soul." I knew his words were an acknowledgment of what I was experiencing. In these "infinite reaches of inner space" I was whole and conscious of Pisti's, Istvan's, and my work together to try to break the code of this terrible dream in ourselves and on the earth. I could see that all around the earth people were doing similar work. I began to realize the implications of this work. I became ecstatic. "Oh, this is a wonderful game! This is a great dream!" I felt the unity and the cooperation of so many souls both in spirit and in matter working to heal the earth.

Then I remembered the earth's condition. I remembered the fragmentation, the competitiveness, the thwarted love, the sorrow, the violence, the dissonance. But Pisti said, "The earth will be healed. It has called the Jackal Healers. It is dreaming its future to itself."

Then I heard Istvan say, "Pisti was here."

Chapter Five

"We need a world-view which shows how our deepest aspirations are related to the essential structure of the universe."

– Dr. Haridas Chaudhuri[1]

In our visions with Pisti, Istvan and I had experienced the realization of some of our deepest aspirations, and through these experiences we understood that those very aspirations were reflections of "the essential structure of the universe." Earlier, from the perspective of severed rational consciousness, I would have asked, "How can individual experience reveal anything about 'the essential structure of the universe'? Isn't this the work of science?" But I now knew that the "universe" was the work both of the private individual and the public scientist. Anything less would be incomplete and incapable of allowing a new worldview to emerge into Western consciousness.

The individual experiences that Istvan and I had, and continued to have, offered us a *knowing* that resonated deep in what felt like the very cellular structure of our bodies. However, in spite of this very real physical groundedness, our experiential perspective often shifted out of our bodies. After the first experience it seemed clear to us that consciousness is not dependent on matter, time or space, but rather that it is in a creative, loving relationship with the physical world. We experienced matter as the infinitely diverse expression of Mind/Spirit in time and space. Gradually we came to realize that thoughts and feelings affect the physical world. Now we understood that the "force behind the force of pure creativity" is Mind itself. Mind *is* Spirit, and it is "the essence of Life."

For Istvan it was as though a floodgate had been opened. Every moment he was alone, he felt Pisti's presence. They communicated as Istvan drove to and from work, they talked in his dreams, and Istvan discovered that if he lay in the "bridge" position of Istvan's vision of Pisti in the hospital, he would go into a deep meditative state in which Pisti was present. Istvan felt as though fifty-five years of his life really had been "put on ice," and that only now was he waking up to the incredible reality of the universe.

The layers of what we had called "normal" life were dissolving. Of course, we still did the normal things. We went to work, we responded to the needs of each day, we talked with our friends, and we grieved the absence of Pisti in this dimension of our lives. But nothing, absolutely nothing, was the same. A multidimensional universe had been opened to us through the death of what we loved most. We had been beckoned into this new life through the gate of dissolution and death—not only of our child but of our entire worldview.

When the form of Anubis, the announcer of death and the conductor of souls to the Great Void, had appeared in our mirror of normality, his energy had shattered this mirror into a thousand fragments. But just as the great sun god Ra had sent Anubis down to piece together the dismembered Osiris, Anubis beckoned us to follow him. As he turned completely around on his own axis, his energy pulled our shattered lives into the vortex of their own fragments. Within this spiraling mass of broken pieces, a different resonance began to emerge. Each fragment would be transformed through the powerful vibration of the organizing principle of life. Our deepest aspirations had magnetically pulled us into the transformative energy of "the essential structure of the universe."

I kept thinking of Pisti's haunting words: "The earth will be healed. It has called the Jackal Healers. It is dreaming its future to itself." Was the earth calling to itself the death of our worldview? Were we, as a culture or an entire planet, ready to confront the mystery of death itself? Of the Void? Of no-thingness and nonbeing? And did we know intuitively that by confronting death—the very principle of the dissolution of all living things—we would curve the straight line of our mythological Imagination into a circle, and with that circle would come the inevitable confrontation with all the *excluded realities* of our present worldview?

Evidently Istvan, Pisti, and I, on some level, were calling our future to ourselves by stepping into the mystery of death. Would Istvan and I be able to hold the "dead end" of this dark, excluded reality without being destroyed? And what did it mean in actual experience to curve the straight line and connect death with birth to create the circle of life? All of us can have some real experience with birth and life, but how can we experience the mystery of death in a conscious and meaningful way so that we can bring these apparent opposites together?

In the ancient world it was this very mystery of death and darkness that was viewed not only as the major spiritual problem but as the experience through which this problem could be solved. Initiation into the Mystery School at Eleusis in ancient Greece was an initiation into the secret of death itself. Those individuals who experienced the mystery of death also experienced the mystery of life: they reconnected the circle and lived life fully without fear.

According to Kerényi, the visionary experience at Eleusis offered such joy and confidence to the individual and the community that participation in the Mysteries was not only "bound up inseparably" with the very existence of Greek life, but it was believed to "hold the entire human race together."[2] Stanislav Grof, founding president of the International Transpersonal Association, reminds us that the rites of the Eleusinian Mysteries were conducted over a period of two thousand years and that more than three thousand people were initiated every five years. This fact, says Grof, reflects the magnitude of influence that Eleusis had "on ancient Greek culture and through it on European culture in general."[3] Its vision, in Kerényi's words, "encompassed and concerned the whole world" because it was a response to that world's spiritual need: "Participation in the Mysteries offered a guarantee of life without fear of death, of confidence in the face of death."[4]

Kerényi says the "secret" that was experienced in this initiation could be expressed in these words: the root aspect of all being is in nonbeing.[5] This obviously could not be understood within a linear thought system. The secret could be stated conceptually, but it remained forever what the German poet Goethe would later call the "Holy open secret":[6] it could be talked about openly, it could be taught, but it could never be "known" until the individual experienced it for one's self. The healing circle could not be formed by institutional knowledge. It could only be formed by individual experience. It was the knowledge beyond books that had been promised by the jackal.

My experience of this "Holy open secret" began after I returned from Peru in 1989. So when the jackal appeared in my dream two years later, just months before Pisti's death, I was already on the path of dissolution and transformation. Seen from this perspective, the jackal was both a confirmation of this process and a harbinger of what was yet to come.

When the first experience came, I was lying on the bed listening to music:

> *I began to laugh uncontrollably. Some long forgotten memory began to flow through my body. Before it reached rational consciousness, I already knew it, knew it in my body, and the cells were laughing with memory. I saw a rather unclear figure move swiftly toward me with definite purpose. I knew she was Paccha Mama, the Old Woman of the Mountain, the source of all being. In less than a second she was no longer to be seen, but I felt her presence and I was back at Machu Picchu. I was up above the mountain looking down at what I knew was my dead body wrapped in canvas and tied with rope. It was on a hospital gurney that was being pushed quietly and quickly by four spiritlike beings. I had no remorse about my death … . Suddenly I saw that I was being pushed toward Huayna Picchu. I was elated. I was to be allowed to enter the holy of holies – the ancient ones would speak to me, mysteries would be revealed to me. But just as suddenly the beings stopped at the entry into the sacred mountain. In a flash everything*

changed. What my body had known from the beginning had finally reached the rational mind. While my body laughed, the images had moved in linear fashion to communicate with the brain. Now all of me remembered. What a joke I had played on myself! I was the mountain, the ancient ones, the Old Woman, the mystery, the Source. I laughed uproariously. Never had I laughed like this before. It was a molecular laugh, a laugh that vibrated in the cells and shot straight through the toe nails, skin, and hair. This was gnosis, that knowing for which no proof is asked because the experience is the knowing – to question it would bring forth more uncontrollable laughter. There was no egotism in the experience, simply memory of who I am, who we all are. Then I saw myself sitting in a forest, and I was surrounded by deer. I heard myself say, "But I can't create a world!" And a voice answered, "You just did create a world in which you cannot create! We can do nothing but create." I knew this, remembered this fully and completely. And with this memory, I flew past Huayna Picchu and spoke my creation: "Then I will create better games, games where all our children will be healed, where all our children will live in a world of ecstasy, joy, love, and peace." As I spoke, I myself was in a state of ecstasy. I was in love with the universe. I knew our world did not have to be as it is. I knew it is what we have created. In the moment this did not make me sad. I was experiencing what we can do, not what we have done. There would be time for sadness later.[7]

Paccha Mama, the Earth Mother, Matter herself, had responded to my deepest aspiration to understand her essence. She led me back to the heart of nature in the sacred mountain where I confronted the Cosmic Mind, the All, not as Other, but as Self. *Here, the very heart of matter revealed herself as Spirit.* This *is* the Great Mystery: matter is spirit, birth and death are transformations within life, and each of us is "the nucleus of the nucleus" of that life.

During the vision I did not fear death. My consciousness, which was above my body, was aware that death and birth are occurring every moment in both the physical and mental worlds.

I was anxious to die to my old limitations and be born into an expanded consciousness. I understood that death and birth are the transformations that connect the two ends of the straight line to form the circle of life. And both are rooted in the All of the Great Void. For the first time, I could understand Kerényi's words: the root aspect of all being is in nonbeing. I also could understand Gandhi's words: "Birth and death are not two different states, but they are different aspects of the same state."

This sacred truth is reflected in the Demeter and Persephone myth that was associated with the transforming experience in the Mystery School at Eleusis. The image of Persephone with her mother Demeter reflects the form of life, while the image of Persephone with her husband Hades reflects the minimal degree of form, which is death. Persephone is deeply bonded to both the mother of life and the husband of death – to form and to nonform. She is one of those mythological buds that, in its unfolding, embodies two forms of being, life and death, "carried to extremes" and exquisitely "balanced against one another."[8] As the initiate enters into the realities of these extremes, the mystery of their deep unity is experienced. This mystery is reflected in the narrative: the very moment Persephone is touched by her husband Death, she conceives new life in her womb, and when she emerges out of the "underworld" of Hades, she brings with her the child born out of death and darkness. The ancients did indeed understand this powerful mystery of death and birth.

And so do modern physicists. This same narrative in matter is called the story of "the quantum vacuum." According to Brian Swimme,

> *The vacuum is everywhere, ... Even where there are no atoms, and no elementary particles, and no protons, and no photons, suddenly elementary particles will emerge. The particles simply foam into existence .... Most of us have Newtonian minds with a built-in prejudice that thinks of the vacuum as dead. If we insist that only material is real and that the vacuum is dead and inert, we will have to find some way to keep ourselves ignorant of this deep discovery by the*

physicists: particles emerge from the "vacuum." They do not sneak in from some hiding place when we are not looking. Nor are they bits of light energy that have transformed into protons. These elementary particles crop up out of the vacuum itself – that is the simple and awesome discovery. I am asking you to contemplate a universe where, somehow, being itself arises out of a field of "fecund emptiness."[9]

Modern physicists also know that each of us is "the nucleus of the nucleus" of the universe. Each person is at the center of the universe and is an integral part of the "flaring forth" of this continuing creative act that began fifteen billion light-years ago with the "Big Bang." Thus, states Swimme, "we are simultaneously at the center of the cosmic expansion and fifteen billion light-years away from the origin of the cosmic explosion."[10] Swimme further explains that

A re-education of the mind is necessary to make sense of what we have discovered .... For we have discovered an omnicentric evolutionary universe, a developing reality which from the beginning is centered upon itself at each place of its existence. In this universe of ours to be in existence is to be at the cosmic center of the complexifying whole.[11]

As we attempt to reeducate our minds with the new perceptions of reality being developed by modern science, we are creating a new worldview that not only has enough space for individual, transformative experience but, in fact, *requires* it. Only the individual experience can curve the straight line into a circle of wholeness. From this perspective, the real death in our culture is not physical death, but the death of this innate knowledge about reality.

Had Istvan and I now called this knowledge back to ourselves? If indeed we had, this call must have come from layers of the mind far deeper than our rational consciousness. At these deep layers the mind functions with the cognition of its own wholeness. That means the mind is able to create in harmony with the organizing principles of dissolution, transformation, and rebirth. This cannot happen, however, if the rational mind has been uprooted from its source in these deep layers. Having lost the knowledge of its wholeness, the initial confrontation with the dissolution of form is experienced as "the jarring end" of everything it had considered "normal."

Neither Istvan, Pisti, nor I had consciously called death and dissolution to ourselves, but the dreams and visions of each one of us before Pisti's death revealed that on these deep levels of mind, we knew it was coming. And in the visions after Pisti's death we realized that, on the same deep levels, we were even co-creating these major events in our lives. Now I could understand that the part of me that had accepted Pisti's death in my earlier dreams was that deep Mind that was in harmony with "the essential structure of the universe." Yet, coexisting with this wisdom was my unaccepting mind that distorted, displaced, and rejected the knowledge that was being communicated to it.

Gradually Istvan and I came to realize that the symbols of the "bridge," which both of us had experienced, were reflections of this deep Mind's creative effort to join what had been separated. The mind's healing energy began to reroot the severed rational mind in the deep layers of its own origins. This allowed us to experience the unity of death and birth. When Istvan had experienced Pisti as this bridge when Pisti was dying in the hospital, the words *life* and *death* had no significance because Istvan knew that "the whole universe was alive." And the jackal, Anubis, was the mythic image of this same experience: the unity of death and birth. When Istvan and I experienced this unity, our Western linear thinking began to curve back into the great circle of life.

As this bridge was forming out of the event in our lives that was the most catastrophic and the most creative, Istvan and I were gradually learning, stumbling though we were, to dance in the Great Round. Our identities were shifting to deep Mind creating our individual selves in time and space. We were now dreaming with the earth because we were the earth. And Pisti's message was that people all over the world were beginning to dream the future of this deep Mind, the future of earth herself.

I thought of the dream (p. 50-51) I had before Pisti's death, the dream of world catastrophe and of people throughout the world beginning to dance the Round Dance to heal the raped heart. I was amazed at the profound interconnectedness between my often forgotten dreams, the events occurring in our lives, and now our experiences with Pisti, all of which were vibrant, living threads weaving themselves within a larger, mythic tapestry. Our conscious minds could not possibly have held all these threads together, yet the pattern existed and we continued to observe the weaving of patterns out of an intelligence far greater than our rational capabilities could claim.

I had experienced earlier, in less personal ways, the workings of this deep Mind in symbolic and mythic structures. During the many years that I taught mythology and the fairy tale, I was consistently amazed, as were the students, by how these works reflected the deep layers of Mind. The intricate patterns within patterns of wisdom were clearly larger than those of any individual author.

Much later I would read William Irwin Thompson's *Imaginary Landscape: Making Worlds of Myth and Science.* He discusses cognitive patterns that go "all the way down to the cellular level."[12] Drawing from the work of such scientists as Manfred Eigen, Humberto Maturana, James Lovelock, Lynn Margulis and Francisco Varela, Thompson discusses how cognitive principles are evident in the organization of all life, from the molecular and cellular levels, as in immune systems, to dreams, visions, myths, fairy tales, and even in evolutionary cultural and mental shifts.

The most interesting aspect of immune systems, according to Varela, is "their cognitive abilities." These systems "recognize molecular shapes, remember the history of encounters of an individual organism, define the boundaries of a molecular 'self,' and make inferences about molecular species likely to be encountered."[13] For scientists like Varela to be able to observe these "cognitive abilities" in the organization of life, an evolutionary mental shift was required. A similar shift is necessary for the rest of us if we are even to "look" at what they are "seeing." However, once we are able to make this shift, the work of these scientists presents us with data that can help us stabilize our new worldview. From this new perspective, cognition is not an unexplainable epiphenomenon of matter, but rather a reflection of Mind that permeates and organizes all life.

The same cognitive organizing principles of Mind that are at work on the cellular and molecular levels of life are also at work in the organization of individual dreams and visions, in cultural myths and fairy tales, and in evolutionary cultural patterns. As with scientists, scholars of mythology and cultural history have also had to experience an evolutionary mental shift to be able to see the interconnected patterns in these imaginal and cultural structures. The more inclusive of the imaginal structures, such as myth and fairy tale, are described by Thompson as documents "of the natural history of life and the cultural history of consciousness."[14] From the perspective of this new worldview, we can "begin to appreciate," in the phenomena we observe, whether on the cellular and molecular levels, the imaginal mental level, or the cultural level, "that nature has such marvelous complexities of immanental mind ... that form can emerge without [individual] 'conscious purpose.'" Such forms are reflections of Mind that is immanent in all life and that "can remember more than it individually knows."[15]

For many earlier cultures, the appreciation of "such marvelous complexities of immanental mind" in nature was the very source of their well-being. This required keeping the rational mind rooted in its own deep layers. In these cultures, therefore, nothing was more important than achieving intuitive consciousness of and maintaining harmony with the organizing principles within the marvelous and complex forms of all life. In Celtic cultures, for example, it was the responsibility of the bards, the storytellers, to maintain harmony and, therefore, "order" in their tribes by aligning themselves with these principles.

The bards did this, says Caitlín Matthews, by becoming "the living memory," the "oral library" of their people. They memorized hundreds of stories—narratives about people, about tribes, and about the universe. They understood that these patterns within patterns were reflections of the spontaneous principles of Mind that permeated all life. The bards were visionaries, musicians, and poets who maintained their attunement with the deep ordering principles of life through their visions, music, and poetry. Since their art was in harmony with immanental Mind, they were able to ignite or transmit this attunement to their listeners. In the Celtic world this magical act of transmission functioned as a kind of *Baraka,* a blessing upon those present. Without Baraka, the Celts knew that their world would lose its *ordered* structure and become a *wasteland.*[16]

Not only did Western culture lose its creative relationship with these principles, it even lost memory of their existence. We became so out of touch with the principles of immanental Mind that "many people can now argue seriously" that these principles do not exist. However, a transformation in our worldview is taking place. Personal experience and scholarly work have led many people to a profound confrontation with these principles. This confrontation has presented them with an opportunity to refocus and look at the empty spaces within the known structures and gradually begin to "see" the excluded realities of our accepted thought system.

Scholars, scientists, artists, mystics and visionaries are among those persons who have experienced this transformation or shift in their worldview. Although their perspectives range from that of the physicist to that of the visionary, all of them have either experienced or observed immanental Mind as the "organization" of all life. Physicist Amit Goswami goes so far as to say that *experience* is essential: the truth that there is "nothing-but-consciousness must be experienced in order to be truly *understood.*" His *experience* brought him into a deeper level of agreement with his mystic friends who held that consciousness is "original, self-contained, and constitutive of all things."[17] This new perspective in physics is the result of such a major "mental shift" that physicist Fred Alan Wolf has remarked that we are experiencing "not only the end of a century but the end of science as we know it."[18] In fact, according to Goswami, "The centerpiece of this new paradigm is the recognition that modern science validates an ancient idea—the idea that consciousness, not matter, is the ground of all being."[19]

When Istvan and I first began to experience this "mental shift," we were not aware that this same shift was occurring in the outer world. Yet our visions consistently reflected the emergence of a new planetary consciousness. Our view of the outer world did not appear to support our visions, but we realized that many of the outer events were the consequences of the old worldview and that we needed to look at that which is coming into being. This gave an even deeper significance to Pisti's dream in which he asked the spirit artist what we can do to heal the earth, and the spirit's answer was to "Protect everything that is coming into being."

After these experiences it was gratifying to read that it is Thompson's position that our civilization is presently "undergoing a transformation of its basic mentality" and moving into a "new planetary culture."[20] Such a change in the worldview of a civilization, says Thompson, does not occur through the exchange of information, "for what is required is not merely the presentation of data and the communication of ideas, but ... a shift in the basic mentality in which data is envisioned and articulated."[21] Nothing could be more accurate or, at times, more discouraging, than the reality that this "shift in the basic mentality" does not take place with the presentation of facts alone—regardless of how many there are or how elegantly rational they may be.

Our basic mentality selects, shapes, frames, and articulates our worldview. To change this process is so difficult that most people, according to Thompson, do not even attempt "that kind of radical transformation within a lifetime."[22] It is far easier to assume that the world we view through our cultural frame is, in fact, "The World."

In spite of this, however, many people are changing and a decisive factor for change is an *experience* of immanental Mind. Grof calls this kind of experience a *non-ordinary state of consciousness*. He states that all those he has known, including scientists, who have had such an experience eventually rejected the materialistic worldview. "They embraced a worldview that describes a radically ensouled universe permeated by Absolute Consciousness and Superior Cosmic Intelligence." Grof believes "that something similar would happen to our entire culture if non-ordinary states became generally accessible."[23] Therefore, he feels that it is especially important to continue research in methods of achieving non-ordinary states of consciousness.

In my own case, I had struggled all my conscious life to find a way of viewing the world outside the limits my culture had established for me. Unfortunately, the frame itself always pulled me back into the prison of its own limitations. I even had powerful experiences of immanental Mind, but I still could not entirely break the frame of my cultural mentality. Until Pisti's death, neither facts *nor* experience could completely shatter the "holding pattern" of my worldview. Only then would Istvan and I experience such "marvelous complexities" of patterns—from the personal to the mythic—that the old limits would be dissolved.

Later, I was deeply moved when I read Swimme's statement that "Indians of South America teach that to become human 'one must make room in oneself for the immensities of the universe'"; otherwise, "we cannot find our true nature."[24] I knew painfully well just how difficult it can be to "make room in oneself" for a universe whose immensities are infinitely creative. But I also felt that as more of us are able to make this shift, it will be easier for those who follow.

Since Istvan and I had experienced these complex patterns emerging out of the structuring forces of the deep layers of Mind, it was exciting to read that Thompson also views the transformation of our culture's "basic mentality" as being orchestrated from within these same deep layers. As this "wave of organization" moves through human consciousness, events, new ideas, and new technologies, says Thompson, emerge together like intricate parts of the "grammar of a language that holds them together in significant ways."[25]

On an individual level, each of us is affected in a different way, and each of us expresses the energy of these structuring forces in the form of our unique interest, whether that is biology, physics, mathematics, economics, art, mythology, theology, archaeology, or any other perspective. While some people are able to articulate this "new mentality," others are not. And, of course, many remain unconscious that a shift is even taking place. Thompson points out that "when one is observing one of these shifts in mentalities, one can learn much from the mystics, crazies, and noisemakers, for they will be performing the new unconscious geometry that no one can yet see."[26]

Although this "new, emerging phenomenon" is being articulated in various fields of research and in individual experience, the overall "landscape," says Thompson, is not yet clearly visible. This greater visibility is necessary if we are to understand the "grammar" that holds these various articulations together in significant ways. However, until more people gain greater understanding of this new, much larger picture, we will see the old cultural frames aggressively assert their rigidity *because of* the presence of these new dynamic forms of consciousness. This is quite natural, even with the most creative among us.

Such was the case with Albert Einstein in 1914. Swimme tells the story of Einstein's astonishment and resistance to his own mathematical calculations that revealed not a fixed and unchanging universe but one that was expanding in all directions:

> *This was not a minor modification. This was an idea that, if true, would shatter the world-view of everyone, Einstein included ... . Can anyone wonder at the fact that Einstein rejected this truth? That he lost his nerve? That he altered the equations to hide their difficult truth? In all this he was only too human, for how many of us are capable of accepting, all at once, the full truth when it comes in the form of a knife? How many of us let it cut through our hold on a false version of reality without first administering some edge-blunting that allows us to cling to one or two accustomed fictions?*[27]

According to Swimme, Einstein would later conclude that "the doctoring of his field equations in order to escape their prediction of an expanding universe represented 'the greatest blunder of my scientific career.'" This conclusion did not come, however, until Einstein was invited to Mount Palomar by the astronomer Edwin Hubble to experience "with his own eyes the galaxies expanding away from us ... ."[28]

Unfortunately, the very history of Western consciousness is shaped by such blunders, but, unlike those of Einstein, these blunders have been collectively maintained for centuries.[29] The result has been a worldview that is not in harmony with the organizing principles of life. This is in sharp contrast to the new worldview that is appearing on the horizon. Since this perspective is in harmony with the organizing principles of life, it cannot be grasped through rational understanding alone. Many who are presently articulating this new worldview are able to do so because of their own exploration in "the inner space and time of consciousness." Such exploration is "a desperately and urgently required project for our time," for at this point in our evolution both rational understanding *and* individual experience are needed for us to create in harmony with these life principles—and thus heal ourselves and our planet.

A major gateway to the experience of this phenomenon is the Imagination. Becoming conscious of the power of the Imagination can be very difficult. As a child, I lived in the realm of the Imagination, but gradually I lost the knowledge of its value. Therefore, as an adult I was not able to appreciate this function of the mind that, according to my culture, is unreliable and "makes up" nonsense. I had to relearn how to approach the Imagination with respect before I could participate in its power.

Laing describes my experience well when he states that "To adapt to this world the child abdicates its ecstasy."[30] Yet Thompson says, "If we come to the edge of our knowing, we have to imagine,"[31] but it is precisely *this* act that we have been trained not to trust. We fear that we are *making up* any image that comes to us. To move beyond this is a matter of patiently deconstructing our culture's trivialized attitude toward the Imagination and retraining ourselves to be attentive to its language.

Thompson provides a helpful image: "The Imagination is like a transformer that takes electricity and steps it down to household current so that it can be used to run the appliances of our daily lives."[32] When we can think of electricity as a metaphor for the unlimited power of the multidimensional Mind and when we can think of the Imagination as our mental capacity to take in this energy and transform it into language, we can then begin to relearn how to use what is truly our "native" language.

For example, now when the Imagination presents my consciousness with an image, a feeling, an intuition, a word—whatever—I acknowledge and observe it. I allow it to fill my mind, and I wait. Sometimes the communication is fast, but at other times it emerges over a period of time. I now respect this process as I would a wise Elder who wishes to communicate with me. And thus, gradually, I have come to accept through experience what earlier I had accepted rationally from my study of Giambattista Vico, a major theorist of symbolic, mythic language: symbolic language is valid and equal to conceptual, rational language. This imaginative language develops before rational thought, and it is out of the poetic logic of this first language that conceptual logic develops.[33] Therefore, imaginative language truly is the voice of our Elders.

Through this language, says Thompson, we may "perceive" realities that our rational minds cannot "conceive." The Imagination, he says, is like "a living membrane between the unknown and the known." It is our "sensitivity to the other dimensions of Mind.... that reconstitutes the inconceivable into the perceivable; ..."[34] Each image or cluster of images is an integral part of a natural system of communication that is structured by the deep principles that organize all life forms. From this perspective, such images and imagistic narratives can be understood as the Imagination's attempt to communicate a reality from another dimension of Mind to individual consciousness. I agree with Dianne Skafte's comment: since Mind is immanent in all life, it would make very good sense that it would create modes of communicating with itself.[35]

Those persons who have been open to the Imagination, such as artists, creative scientists, and other types of imaginative thinkers, have experienced the *logic* of dreams, reveries, and visions, which they later translated into art, scientific theories, mathematical calculations, and other forms of conceptual language. Thompson points out that Einstein and Tesla were among those scientists in whom this "hieroglyphic mode of thought" was particularly pronounced.[36] Such persons, he says, understand that

> *Mind is indeed larger than ideologies or world views and as we become sensitive to multidimensionality at the edge of our limited forms of perception, we may register the images that are metaphors for the knowledge that is coming to us from all the other dimensions beyond the three we have habitually constituted as our "world."*[37]

The more experience Istvan and I had in these interpenetrating worlds, the more we understood what Pisti meant when he said that the earth would be healed because it had called the Jackal Healers to itself. Our own deepest aspirations to be healed were intricately connected to those same aspirations throughout the world. We now understood that all personal narratives are woven within the great web of cultural and mythic narratives, and that the roots of all truly creative narratives are deep in immanental Mind.

The German poet Novalis understood that "Every person's life is a sacred text."[38] As we follow the threads of our deepest aspirations to their source in "the essential structure of the universe," we begin to see just how sacred each life is and how it connects to the whole, the vast whole of all life. As Thompson says, "when wholes are invoked they bring with them 'the patterns that connect,' the patterns of narrative, story, and myth … .Technical thinking is narrow and specialized, but mythic thinking is macrothought. Think big and you think myth."[39]

The earth is thinking big. It is giving birth to a worldview that will allow us to see how our deepest aspirations really are related to "the essential structure of the universe." We are dreaming the straight line into a circle—and we are dreaming big. We are dreaming a new myth.

Chapter Six

"Live each moment fully. Then let it go."

—Pisti

Following our first visions after Pisti's death, Istvan and I participated in two worlds. One was the world in which Pisti was no longer physically present. The other was the world of Mind, of presence and creativity. Here the unique consciousness of Pisti was present, but always within the context of his larger creating Self. He, as Pisti, was like a living work of art in a large mosaic that fit into an even larger artistic design.

Once I felt him say to me, "Think of my life as a painting." Together we looked at this painting, and I understood the *artistic necessity* of its basic composition. That is, I was able to have at least some understanding of the organizing principle working in his life to help him realize the intention that gave him birth. However, I also was able to see how the collective nature of creativity complicates the achievement of these intentions. Once again I realized how important it is to "Protect everything that is coming into being."

This experience reminded me of the image of the old man who, in my dream before Pisti's birth, had created the painting of the young man I knew would be born as my son. As I pondered this image of the old man sitting in the rocking chair and smoking his pipe, the image began to take on a life of its own. I watched the man slowly and calmly inhale the smoke. As he exhaled, I saw the smoke divide into separate streams of intention and flow out in many directions. Each stream of smoke manifested itself in a living, conscious work of art. Some of the creations remained in Mind while others materialized in time and space.

Sometimes the power and vastness of this creativity undid me, and I fell back into the world where I was Pisti's mother, where he was dead, and where we would never be together again. After all, this world also had its reality.

I knew that this world's *reality* was our *perception* of the world that we had historically constructed and collectively maintained. I knew this—even while I experienced its paralyzing effect on me. It was clear that my personal work was to deconstruct these trained modes of perception within my own mind. I was grateful that there was evidently a part of me that always lived in the wisdom of Mind, that knew and understood the process of deconstruction and creation that was working within me. Yet the tension between the two worlds was real and would continue to be real until the creative principles of Mind could flow through me without being intercepted and garbled into the tangled shape of our present worldview.

One afternoon, when I felt frozen in that empty, garbled world, I decided to get out of the house and go to a bookstore. As I browsed through the books, I was unaware of the music that was being played until suddenly my attention was captivated by a piece I had never heard. I sat down and attempted to appear normal, but I felt something open in my heart. The sorrow was overwhelmingly intense, but, strangely, so was the joy. When the music finished, I put the book I was reading back on the shelf, purchased the tape of music, and left the store. I was amused that the piece was called *Miracles*.[1]

Later that evening I decided to listen to the music again. I placed the tape in the stereo in Pisti's room and went into my bedroom to change clothes. As I stepped out of my sweats, I was once again overcome by the music. I looked at the pictures of Pisti on the dresser, and suddenly my perspective started to distance itself from everything in front of me. My consciousness seemed to be leaving the room and moving toward the music while my body stood still. I quickly followed "myself" into Pisti's room, closed the door, and lay down on the bed in the darkness.

The moment I closed my eyes, I felt Pisti's presence so strongly that I was startled. I felt him say, "Let's look at all my forms as Pisti. Let's live through them together." I began to remember him as a baby and then as a very young boy. Soon I was no longer just remembering. I was inside specific moments. While my consciousness fully participated in this past, it was also strangely "located" slightly up in the air to my right where Pisti and I were "surfing" the great creative waves of life together. These waves were energetic and vigorous. One could sink and drown, be ripped apart, or skillfully ride the waves in a state of ecstasy.

Down on the bed I was crying, laughing, then frantically trying to hold onto the moment—to make it last just a little longer. At such times, I began to sink. Then I could hear Pisti say, "Live each moment fully. Then let it go." These were the critical periods of excruciating tension between holding on and letting go. Then, when I released everything to save myself from drowning, I felt myself rise high on the crest of the life force. It was exhilarating. In these moments I knew how deadly and unnecessary it was to try to hold onto anything. After all, here we were, Pisti and I, alive, participating, observing, and creating together on the vast, eternal ocean of Mind.

Then I returned to time and space. Pisti was a young man. I saw him smile. Pain shot through my heart. I would never see him smile again. I heard Pisti say, "We can always create that smile again." But I knew that would be another life, another time, and another space. I felt myself sinking, but I could still hear Pisti's coaching: "Flow with time. Surf with time. Surf on the great force of life."

As I saw the high school years coming, we both began to laugh. I said I could let go of those years very well. The moment I had this thought, we were living the last years of his life. I felt his joy, his love, his deep desire to create a life of meaning and purpose. And I felt my own relief and happiness that he had made it through the difficult years. Then, abruptly, I landed in the final month—the accident, the days in the Trauma Center. I leaned over his beautiful image and kissed the middle of his forehead. The combined energy of all his images returned. No. I would not let him go.

But, I thought, he has already died, and here we are together. His consciousness filled the room, yet I stood frozen in this last moment. Slowly, Pisti said, "Remember Faust. Remember that it is precisely when he cries out, 'Linger, linger, [this moment] thou art so beautiful!' that he can fall into the power of Mephistopheles." In that exact instant the music was finished. I sat up. The conflict was gone. I realized that something deep in me was in the process of relinquishing the material forms of Pisti. This was occurring, not because I was unusually courageous or strong, but because I had experienced the essence that created those forms. I felt a pervasive peace flow through my mind and body. I lay back down on the bed. I looked out at the stars. I was in awe of the universe.

I thought about what it really means to live each moment fully with open hands, to love deeply and, at the same time, to be able to relinquish it all. This, if anything, requires the exquisite balance of Persephone, she who is bonded through love both to the mother of life and to the husband of death, to form and to nonform. I had been bonded to form, but I could not be bonded to nonform until I had consciously experienced it. I, like Persephone, had to be abducted by the Lord of the Great Void. Anubis, the jackal, had opened the way to the powerful love and creativity in the essence of all life. Now I also belonged to both worlds—but I was still learning how to walk between these worlds in harmony and in balance, how to weave them together into one dynamic, living fabric.

I could see that Persephone is a sacred image of immanental Mind: she reflects life that is lived in balance and harmony with the principles that organize, dissolve, and recreate all life. Now the deep layers of my mind were giving birth to Persephone in me. I had experienced how letting each moment go allowed me to surf the waves of life in a state of ecstasy. Pisti was teaching me to let him go in material time and space so I could experience more fully his essence in "the inner space and time of consciousness." It was becoming apparent that this balance of Persephone, as well as that of the jackal, was the "Opener of the Way" to multi-dimensional consciousness.

I laughed when I remembered that the music was called *Miracles*. I had, indeed, experienced a *miracle*. As I thought about the definition of this word as an event that *appears* to contradict the known laws of science, I marveled at how such events must always be taking place around us, in us, and throughout this infinitely creative universe. Surely no science, however advanced, could ever include all the laws of creativity. I wanted to stay open to such events even though they appeared to contradict what we have agreed is reality. I certainly knew that my experience of Pisti's absence in the world of matter was real, yet equally real was my experience of his presence in the world of Mind. This meant respectfully holding these apparent contradictions in a state of balance so that what I now perceived as two worlds could be experienced as one dynamic process of ebb and flow, of birth and death, of absence and presence, of darkness and light, of inner and outer, of matter and spirit.

In the meantime, however, Istvan and I were very concerned about Jenny. She had been devastated by Pisti's death. While she was convinced that Pisti's consciousness was continuous, his absence was her daily reality. She was fortunate to have a loving and understanding family who did everything they could to help her through the grief she was experiencing. They knew that her life was profoundly changed. I often wondered whether it was more painful to lose a child to death or to lose a child to grief.

Istvan, Jenny, and I were often together during the first two years following Pisti's death. We went to Hungary together to visit Pisti's Hungarian grandmother and our many other relatives in that country. We also carried Pisti's ashes to Mount Baldy, where Pisti and Jenny had spent so much time together, and to Mount Shasta and Sedona. A few weeks before Pisti's accident he had said to Jenny and a few of their friends that if one were to die, the truly wonderful thing would be to have one's ashes scattered at sacred places on the earth. When Pisti died, the three of us vowed to do just that. And that first spring Jenny took my class in mythology and symbolic language. After class we often spent hours talking over coffee. Sometimes she would come by our house to meditate in Pisti's room. It was there that she too stepped into the multidimensional world of immanental Mind.

Her experiences in "the inner space and time of consciousness" formed the path that brought Jenny back to life and balance. The first time she had such an experience, she said she wanted to run out of his room and tell us that he wasn't dead, that not only was he creating with us but that he was creating in other dimensions as well. "But," she said, "I didn't dare move. I wanted to experience him as much and as long as I could." The following description of her experience is from her journal and notes in her words that I wrote down at that time:

> *At first I know that Steve (Pisti) is present, but there is no image. I wait. Then I see a sandy beach and the ocean. Now Steve and I both have bodies, but they are spirit forms, sort of transparent, yet I am able to see if I choose to see. I can see all other physical forms. Everything is still and beautiful.*
>
> *I am so excited because I know he isn't dead and we are together again. He picks me up and runs into the ocean with me. We hold each other for a long time. It is so personal and real. Finally, we are sitting on the beach together, and he says, "I have so much to tell you."*
>
> *Then we go together into lush mountains and then out into space. I look down, and I can see the earth. Steve wants to show me the disease of the planet. He says the illness is getting worse – both in human beings and in the environment. I can see the dirt and pollution all around the earth. I realize that this is a spirit picture from space. The earth is so small, but we can see the damage we have done to it. I realize that this kind of pollution gets in the way of our communication with "the other side." He encourages me to take care of my body, to nourish it and to nourish the earth and its precious resources, to love myself and to love the earth.*

When Jenny told Istvan and me about this experience, Istvan related to Jenny the similar vision of the earth that he had experienced. This was a powerful moment for all three of us: Pisti was urgently focusing our attention on the stressed condition of the earth and the role the human species plays in that condition.

Jenny said that this part of the vision was a surprise to her because she had not been conscious of the seriousness of the problem before this experience. She felt such love coming from Pisti for her and for the earth. He talked with her in detail about taking care of herself emotionally and physically. Jenny now understood that taking care of herself was the first step toward taking care of her larger body, which was the earth.

I wanted to tell everyone about these amazing journeys into "the inner space and time of consciousness," but I soon realized what I was up against. The same struggle with doubt, denial, and outright rejection that I had experienced in myself now stood before me in the images of friends with whom I thought I could share these experiences. These friends were like mirrors for my own rational mind in its effort to deny and destroy any experience that contradicted its accepted view of reality. Yet they were my friends, people who loved and trusted me. I knew they wanted to be supportive, but they could not be if I continued to inject the disorganizing principle of these experiences. There were, of course, other friends who could and did listen to the stories, but it soon became clear that such experiences are difficult to hold in consciousness if there is not a worldview into which they can fit. Istvan talked with only a few people, and Jenny, quiet and private as she was, talked with no one for a very long time. She simply *knew* that what she had experienced was another dimension of reality, that she could not have understood it without experiencing it, and, therefore, there was no possibility of sharing it.

The three of us realized that Pisti was trying to awaken in us a worldview into which our experiences would not only fit but would be understood as natural expressions of the essence of that worldview. Pisti worked with us in the mode of an ancient Celtic Bard in his effort to awaken our deep memory, to ignite our intuitive, artistic consciousness, to create the conditions necessary for Baraka to magically and spontaneously occur in us. In our dreams and visions he miraculously appeared and told us stories, showed us images, joked with us (especially with Istvan), danced, played haunting music, and we created living, visionary narratives in which he and we participated. He communicated with the greatest urgency that our world had lost its intuitive consciousness of the creative principles that organize and balance the marvelous and complex forms of all life. We had lost our "ordered" structure, and the world had become a "wasteland."

One evening I dreamed I saw Pisti dancing wildly and yet effortlessly out of the North and into the room where I was sleeping. His arms and legs, hands and feet were flying through the air in perfect harmony with a music I could feel but could not hear. His every muscle vibrated with this unheard music. When I was able to see his feet more clearly, I realized that he was dancing in the snakeskin boots he had liked so much. I began to feel the pure joy his presence brought into the room, and, as he continued to dance, I felt him say, "Dance life in snake boots!"

When I awoke, I remembered a conversation Pisti and I had one afternoon about the symbolism of the snake. He had invited me into his room to see two beautiful rattlesnake skins he had just hung on his wall. The snakes had been run over on Mount Baldy, and Pisti had skinned them. I mentioned that people of the ancient world had viewed the snake as a powerful manifestation of the divine and that they had honored the sacred mystery of death and birth in the snake's ability to shed its dead skin and allow the soft, new skin to come into being.

I wanted to be able to dance life in snake boots, to be able to release the dead forms so that the new forms could live in me. I had experienced the exuberance and joy this ability releases. All three of us wanted this. Istvan, Jenny, and I wanted to do whatever was necessary to allow this new vision to be born in us. We understood that we needed to heal ourselves of the damage of our present worldview and to learn how to heal our larger selves, the earth, of this same damage. We wanted to achieve a balance in our lives and to extend our connectedness with this multidimensional world. We continued to be attentive to our dreams, our waking visions, and our precognitive and synchronistic experiences. Sometimes we did not understand what we were going through, but we recorded everything, the chaos as well as the order, with as much detail and accuracy as we possibly could. Another world had opened to us, and we wanted to be good cartographers.

Istvan and I spent most of our free time talking about our experiences, listening to music, reading and meditating. We studied different forms of meditation, and we used techniques from some of the ancient shamanic traditions of Mexico and South America. We felt comfortable and strangely familiar with these traditions because they connected us to nature and to the earth. Gradually we each settled into the form of meditation that suited us individually, and we discovered our own particular needs.

Jenny needed to be in nature, especially in the mountains where she had spent so much time with Pisti. I discovered that my body needed to move with music in a form of dancing meditation, and Istvan, in addition to meditation, discovered books: he read more in the next two years than he had read during his entire life. For several months Istvan meditated lying down in the panther position, which was the "bridge" position of Istvan's vision of Pisti in the hospital. When that no longer worked for him, he used another form of meditation. He often meditated in Pisti's room, but from time to time I would hear him blissfully snoring. When I kidded him about this, he laughed and reminded me of my own words, that "this world also had its reality." This happened so often, however, that we finally came to use the Hungarian word for meditation, *meditacio*, for *nap*. Istvan insisted that this was his own personal technique for keeping the "balance."

After his *meditacio* one Sunday afternoon, Istvan emerged from Pisti's room to tell me a dream he had just had in which Pisti showed him a film. He sat down at the table, folded his arms in front of him, and closed his eyes. I sat down quietly and waited. Something big was happening inside Istvan. I looked at his face and watched the tears push through his closed lashes. His folded arms seemed to hold him in this time and this space. I did not feel it was sadness that Istvan was experiencing, but rather something so profound, so sacred, that he could not speak.

And we did not speak that afternoon about the dream. Only later that evening as we lay in bed, neither of us able to sleep, did I urge him to try to tell me what he had experienced. Then he explained how, during the dream, he felt as though he "understood everything." Yet, later, when he wanted so much to tell me, he simply could not speak. This is what he finally did say:

> *I saw universes creating themselves, absorbing themselves, and recreating themselves – but not necessarily in that order. It all seemed to be happening simultaneously. There was only Now. Everything was energy, but this energy was love. This love was so powerful that it shot out of itself as material worlds, universes, but no matter how much it expanded or changed its forms, it could never lose itself because there was nothing but itself. I experienced this from the inside out, from the heart, but I had the mind of a physicist and was able to understand what I was seeing. Pisti said that I would not be able to hold onto this kind of knowledge when I woke up, but he said that there are physicists and other scientists on the earth now who are beginning to understand some of the basic principles of life that have not been understood in the past.*
>
> *There was so much, but I don't have the words. Instead of just part of me experiencing the film, all of me was experiencing it, but somehow I was the film, Pisti, myself and everything in the film, and all of that was experiencing "it" at once.*
>
> *Pisti told me that consciousness on the earth is going through a powerful transformation. He said that there is now enough energy on the earth, that is, love and longing for love, to hold the beam of light that is coming – whatever that means. I understood it in the dream. What I do remember is that light is energy that is conscious and loving, but it was more than that. Pisti also said that the new child of the human species will have another ring of DNA. Maybe that was a symbol, some way to tell me that the children of the future will be born knowing*

what we are struggling to understand. I felt that if we can heal ourselves, we can give them this gift.

All that night I lay close to Istvan's body. His telling of the dream had created such vast spaces in me that I felt a need to be grounded in the present moment. Once again I had been undone by the vast and powerful creativity of the universe. I longed for Pisti to be present in the material world of time and space. I longed for the known world, the familiar world—with all its limitations. It was true that I wanted to make room in myself for "the immensities of the universe," but tonight it seemed to me that my relationship to these immensities could only exist through my love for the individual forms here in my time and my place.

I knew Pisti's essence existed even though he was no longer in the body. I had experienced his presence, his love, his consciousness, but now, this evening, I felt such a need to *see* him, to see his earthly form. I had trouble sleeping, and when I did sleep, I had strange, confusing dreams. Finally, in the early morning I dreamed Pisti came home. He walked into the kitchen where I was making breakfast. I could see him clearly. He was wearing the white Tibetan shirt he loved, jeans, and his old, dirty Nikes. I asked why he was wearing his old shoes when I had bought him new ones before he died. He smiled and asked me in return, "Am I real enough?" We both laughed at his joking response to my need as we embraced each other. I was prepared to feel empty space, but much to my surprise, he was solid, and I was not.

That morning before Istvan left for work, he made coffee, brought it into the bedroom, and sat down. I told him the dream. I explained how I had longed for the particular, and I got it, right down to the dirty shoes. But I had been in for a surprise: Pisti had walked into the dream as a trickster Bard. What was "real" anyway? Pisti appeared in a very clear, specific image, but did such an image make him more real? Was an image ever more real than the presence of love and consciousness? Even in the dream I did not expect the image to have substance, yet the image was solid and I was empty space. My very "real" material body had no substance at all. But was *it* not real? Then, suddenly, I realized that Pisti's old, worn-out shoes were probably a symbol of the old, worn-out image that I thought I needed. I was not dancing in snake boots.

As Istvan and I talked about the dream, I was reminded once again of the quotation on Pisti's pen and ink drawing: "Listen to the force behind the force of pure creativity. It is the essence of Life." As we talked about this quotation, Istvan and I began to realize that it had become the theme of our journeys into "the inner space and time of consciousness." Istvan said that he now felt that if a person stayed centered in the "essence," there would be no question about what is real. Everything is real, whether it has form or not. Suddenly, the word "listen" took on new meaning. If we could remember to *listen* to the force behind the force that creates all forms, perhaps then we really could "Live each moment fully. Then let it go."

I realized that I had been overwhelmed with the vastness of Istvan's dream because I had not been centered in the essence, the heartfelt source, as Istvan had been. I was overwhelmed by too much form, and I longed for the one beloved form that I had lost. As we talked, I felt an urgent need to look more closely at Pisti's drawing of Dali and himself where this quotation appeared. I jumped out of bed, ran into Pisti's room, and removed the drawing from the portfolio.

I took it back to Istvan, and we looked at it together. While I had seen the background before, I had not really taken it in. Now I saw that the entire design bursts forth from a central point and emanates outward in ever larger, somewhat geometrical shapes. Dali's and Pisti's forms are a part of this bursting forth. Integrated into the background shapes are the words "Élan Vital." They are shaped to give the impression of a powerful resonance coming from the center. Istvan said that he had never really paid attention to the background either. "Now," he said, "after our experiences, it's impossible not to see it, but," he asked, "what is 'Élan Vital'?" I only knew that it was from Henri Bergson's philosophy and that it meant "vital force," so I quickly looked it up in the dictionary, and together we read: "the original vital impulse which is the substance of consciousness and nature."

This is the moment of Baraka:
all worlds are One, and its essence dances in every atom.
Live this moment fully. It is so beautiful.

Chapter Seven

"... there is an angle of experience
where the dark is distilled into light ...."
—Christopher Fry[1]

At the time that Istvan and I were experiencing the essence of Mind flowing in and through all reality, I was also experiencing a darkness that was so painful that I could not bear to speak directly about it even with Istvan. It was not that I was still intercepting the creative principles of Mind and allowing them to be garbled into the tangled shape of our present worldview, but rather that I was inside the horror of such a worldview. The World Child of the Chaco Canyon dream returned, and everywhere I looked, I saw him. He summoned me with his dark eyes to follow him deep into the darkness we have created on this planet.

When I opened the newspaper or turned on the television, I received news of his death, torture, suicide, murder, abandonment. He appeared in the addict, the zealot, the indifferent. I saw his eyes in the murderer, hardened, detached, no longer lovable. I was seeing, hearing, and knowing with an intensity I had never experienced. Whenever this wounded child appeared, I felt as though I were that child's mother. Sometimes, in dreams, the World Child looked at me with Pisti's face, and I woke up grateful that Pisti was already dead. I realized that Pisti's death had dissolved the filter that had regulated the degree of empathy I could endure without my balance being threatened.

I felt I was standing at the edge of an abyss: I knew I could lose my balance and fall, but I also knew that I would not. I was determined to walk through this experience consciously, even though there were times when I prayed to be released from the terrible knowledge it gave me. I knew that if I could tell Istvan, he could help me, but I feared that telling him would catapult us into some parallel world where we would find ourselves living the very realities that I was mourning. I knew this fear was irrational, but still the fear remained.

As painful as these experiences were, I was well aware that I was not the actual mother. Yet the fear that I—or any other mother—could have been, brought me as close to those worlds as I could go without being destroyed. I struggled to hold these experiences consciously before me because I knew that they were not random: the World Child was determined to reveal to me how the consciousness of this planet had shattered its soul.

I came to accept all that Istvan and I were going through as sacred rituals of experience that had to be powerful enough and inclusive enough to frame our potential wholeness and, at the same time, our negation of that wholeness. I felt that my work was to allow myself to experience fully whatever came to me and eventually, as I was able, to put each experience into its place within the frame of this great puzzle. At the time of many of the events, I was not able to perceive their multilayered relatedness. It was sometimes months or even years later that I was able to see how each event fit into this puzzle.

What is astonishing to me now as I look back years later is the degree to which both Istvan and I were working with Pisti on this puzzle. Before Pisti's death I could not have imagined such a reality. Now it was clear that all three of us had been committed to the same "desperately and urgently required project for our time." We were exploring "the inner space and time of consciousness" in search of an "angle of experience where the dark is distilled into light."

Since that December afternoon in my childhood when I heard talk among the adults of a world at war, I had been initiated, step by step, into this world whose darkness seemed far more powerful than its light. Those early years were shaped by my personal life of order and love and by the completely contrasting images of destruction and suffering presented as "news." When I grew older, I learned more about the betrayal and cruelty, the torture and murder, the sorrow and shattering of lives that had occurred in many other parts of the world during my childhood. How, I wondered, could one side of the cultural tapestry appear in such ordered and loving forms while the underneath side revealed such destruction and despair?

This question was painfully intensified when I did the research for my doctoral dissertation on the thought structures of Western consciousness. By looking through the lens of European thought systems, I was gradually able to see that there were two very different systems: one maintained dominance except for short intervals during which the other was tolerated until it was perceived as a threat. Then it was brutally suppressed. The first was an exclusive dominator system, the other an inclusive egalitarian system. The dominator system confronted the "dark" with violence in its attempt to destroy all opposition and to "purify" its own system. The inclusive system confronted the "dark" with perceptions and techniques to distill the dark into light, to transform self and other.

The combined power of State and Church kept this exclusive system of beliefs, practices, and ideas in a dominant position for centuries. When Christianity became the state religion, in the words of Karen Jo Torjesen, the "radically egalitarian ... social revolution" of Jesus was "marginalized."[2] All other modes of thought, worship, and practice were forbidden. In the latter part of the fourth century, the Roman emperor Theodosius issued laws against the continued celebration of the ancient Mysteries,[3] and the possession of books that had been denounced as heretical by the Church now became a criminal offense against the State.[4] All opposition was forced underground.

However, in spite of the fact that there was such strict control of the outward expression of contrary thought and experience, there were periods of relative tolerance when these underground forces could begin to surface. According to John Boswell's major study of tolerance and suppression in European history, the institutions that held power determined how much permissiveness could be allowed without their own dominance being threatened. Where there was no perceived threat to power, there was tolerance. Obviously, freedom of this nature did not come about because bigotry, prejudice, and fear were absent. These predispositions remained very much alive, like a virus that could be triggered by a variety of conditions. Whatever the condition, if it was perceived as a serious threat, institutional power moved against it.[5]

These perceived threats to power and the desire for increased power resulted in (1) the intensified subordination of women; (2) the crusades (1095-1450's) initiated by the Christian Church of western Europe to take possession from the Muslims of The Holy Sepulchre and ultimately to wage war against anyone who was not a Christian under the control of the Western Church;[6] (3) the "Albigensian Crusade" (1209-1244) in which European men, women, and children were killed on "so terrible a scale that it may well constitute the first case of 'genocide' in modern European history." The wealth, sophistication, and independence of the "heretical" culture of southern France was destroyed;[7] (4) the formation of the Inquisition, formally established in 1233, which accused, ruthlessly interrogated, imprisoned, and executed thousands whose thoughts, practices, and beliefs did not adhere to established power;[8] (5) the destruction of the independent and powerful Order of the Knights Templars on charges of "blasphemy and heresy,"[9] "sorcery and deviant sexuality";[10] (6) the brutal colonization of the Americas, beginning in the fifteenth century, which brought about the reduction in population of the indigenous peoples, in the words of Anne Llewellyn Barstow, "from eighty million to about ten million in less than a century, ... the greatest massacre in history"; (7) the enslavement of "somewhere between eleven million and fifteen million Africans in the three centuries of the Atlantic slave trade ... the largest forced movement of people in history."[11] And back home in Europe, (8) Spanish Jews and Moors were faced with conversion and/or expulsion, and (9) at least two hundred thousand people, mainly women, were charged with witchcraft and/or sexual intercourse with the Devil. The dominant powers of Europe, says Barstow, had turned against their own women: thousands were humiliated, imprisoned, tortured, and murdered in "the greatest [European] mass killing of people by people not caused by war, ..."[12] Anyone thought to differ with the dominant powers had been silenced and stripped of independence. And all other spiritual traditions and cultures, including the indigenous spiritual tradition of Europe that had been nurtured by women for centuries, were brutally suppressed.

This research on the violence of the exclusive dominator system allowed me to see that the genocide and torture that was occurring during my childhood were not an anomaly in European history. This brutal violence was, in fact, part of the dominant pattern of behavior that moved across Europe and into the Americas in wave after wave of persecution, expulsion, torture, and murder. The knowledge of this paralyzing darkness reveals the extent to which the dominator system will go to protect its sense of power and its view of reality.

The powers of Europe convinced themselves again and again that they were destroying, or at least controlling, the "darkness" in the world. They sought to destroy "the other" whose ideas, practices, beliefs, race, gender were seen as inferior, dangerous, or worthless. They were able to keep at bay any questions about the darkness within themselves while they battled fiercely against the "evil" and "chaos" they perceived in the outer world. This refusal to become conscious and thus responsible for their own individual darkness perpetuated a cycle of repression and violence.

Yet, during the entire span of this history, there existed within Europe the other, inclusive thought system that held the knowledge of how to confront this repressed darkness and distill it into light. This knowledge is part of the perennial wisdom of the planet, and it was nurtured in the various streams of the underground tradition in Europe. How was it, then, that century after century, wave after wave of darkness, Europe never availed itself of this healing perspective?

Many people did struggle to bring this perspective into European consciousness. During each period of institutional tolerance, this underground perspective emerged and influenced the formation of new social, intellectual, and spiritual attitudes.

This perspective entered consciousness through dreams and visions, through folk culture, through the discovery and translation of ancient texts, through contact with Sufi mysticism, through the revival of the ancient Bardic tradition, through the reemergence of the Hermetic arts, including alchemy, and through the Jewish Kabbalah. This inclusive and unifying perspective initiated the great creative periods in Western history, such as the High Middle Ages, the Renaissance, the Rosicrucian Enlightenment, the High Romantic period, and the present time.[13]

Unfortunately, this perspective never was allowed its full development. Whenever institutional power perceived a threat to its own mode of control, this healing knowledge was brutally and relentlessly suppressed. By the end of the High Romantic period in the nineteenth century, the materialistic paradigm had become strong enough to prevent the wisdom of this underground tradition from being integrated into the mainline tradition of Western culture. Thus political and military power was no longer needed to subdue the excluded realities of European consciousness.

My own understanding of this darkness in European history had been from the perspective of the victim. This view was incomplete, however, and my psyche had a painful surprise in store for me. It is clear to me now that once we step into that "inner space and time of consciousness" with a commitment to heal ourselves and to explore new worlds, there are no limits to the Mind's ability to construct situations, both within and without, that will allow us to experience precisely what we need to know. Mind is concerned with the wholeness of life, and when we enter its vast space and time, we must take on the quality of that wholeness.

Not long after the reappearance of the World Child, I began to have dream experiences of myself in European history as a perpetrator of precisely those crimes that I had perceived only from the perspective of a victim. My mind was shocked by this new image of itself. Nevertheless, it took hold of these experiences and shaped them into a living reality. I began to allow this "knowledge" of the perpetrator as myself rather than "other" to live in me.

While I was still unable to speak with anyone about my experiences with the World Child, I could talk with Istvan about the perpetrator. After telling him the dreams, I said, "Suppose that in various lives during the history of Europe I had been the very perpetrator of those crimes that I have spent this life studying in grief and shock from the perspective of the victim. How clever of the soul," I raved, "how clever and horrible to create such a narrative to heal itself!"

Istvan had always respected my sanity, but he looked at me now with more than a little amazement. "Kicsi,* don't you think you're taking these dreams a little too seriously?" "No," I answered, "not if we look at what taking them seriously might allow me to experience." Istvan was silent. I too was silent because I did not yet know where this experience was leading me.

A few days later, when we talked again, I said to Istvan, "All I know for sure is that the destructive reality of European history cannot be grasped through scholarship alone. Nor can it be understood only from the perspective of the victim. Something in me is moving toward a deeper knowledge of the perpetrator, and this is painful because I feel I am being asked to make room in myself for a darkness I do not wish to claim."

That same evening I thought about an experience that had occurred during Pisti's high school years when he had been struggling with addiction. All of us were trying to bring about healing. My mind had been in such a state of extreme tension that, as I tried to meditate, I felt a circle of women around me. They were "Spirit Women" from around the world. They spoke in one voice: "You are worried about Pisti, but you are the biggest addict in the family. *You are addicted to ordinary consciousness, which is the source of all addictions.* If you will be healed, Pisti will be healed."

---

* Pronounced Kee´chee.

I had been too disturbed that evening to discuss this with Istvan. I went to bed. Throughout the night I felt as though I was neither awake nor asleep but in some zone of unfamiliar clarity. I remembered wondering on that very day how it could be that a person would continue to do something that he knew was harmful to himself. Then I felt as though my mind wrote this question on a blackboard in front of me and proceeded to take me through a review of my own addictive behavior. I observed myself repeatedly seeking realities beyond the rational, material world. In each instance that I experienced these realities, my rational mind fell on them as though they were prey, ripped them apart, and denied their reality with the self-righteous justification of the true academic. Then the longing for these experiences returned: if I could have just one more experience, I would trust it; I would know it is real.

As my mind returned from the memory of that powerful "spiritual intervention" and connected it now with the experiences of seeing myself in the role of the perpetrator, it was clear that the only way I could have become conscious of the seriousness of my own culturally sanctioned and celebrated addiction was for me to identify with the extreme consequences of this addiction in European history. I had not been called, after all, to take responsibility for those specific crimes, but, rather, for the root of those crimes within my own addicted mind. This was the darkness I had to claim.

This perpetrator, disguised as reason, had indeed been alive in me, ever ready to negate any experience of "the immensities of the universe." As I thought of how each experience was attacked and mutilated, the image of Lavinia in Shakespeare's *Titus Andronicus* came to mind as a reflection of my own and my culture's response, not only to the symbolic, visionary mind but to the very open and exploratory nature of reason itself. Lavinia was gang raped by the sons of a man her father had captured in war. To prevent her from telling her story, they cut out her tongue. To prevent her from writing her story, they cut off her arms. Still Lavinia was not defeated: she took a stick by her teeth and scratched her story in the earth. But even those scratchings have been ridiculed, ignored, or denied. In some people, Lavinia no longer even remembers that she has a story to tell.

I had sought Lavinia all my life, and yet I had rejected her repeatedly. Even while I abused her, I longed to hear her story. I recalled the dream of the rapist that I had a few months before Pisti's death. On one level, the rapist was indeed the harbinger of the death of my own child. Now, however, I could see another dimension to this dream. When I thought about how the rapist touched my hand and spoke my name as I groaned in fear and agony, I could not escape the feeling that he—a part of myself—was calling me to awaken to the reality of the rapist in my own mind. As gentle as he was in that moment, I knew he would still rape me. Yet there must have been something in him that longed for healing, just as there always had been in me.

For myself, the Western mind, and now most of the world, it is Lavinia—tongueless, armless, raped, partially conscious at best—who waits for us at the door to multidimensional awareness. Before we can enter that door, we must hear Lavinia's story. We need to know that our failure to experience these dimensions is not because they do not exist, but because we have denied Lavinia the means to communicate with us in her full power.

A much deeper understanding of my dream of world catastrophe was also now available to me. Lavinia's heart had been raped, and the world was in urgent need of healing. Lavinia had scratched her story in the earth for me to see, and the World Child, her child, had summoned me to follow him into the heart of darkness. Here, in this darkness, this Child was both the raped and the rapist. He showed me how the limited consciousness of this planet had shattered his soul, had compelled him to adapt to our meager worldview, had forced him to abdicate his ecstasy.

Just as we also had been forced to abdicate our ecstasy.
Just as we also had been shattered.
Could we, I wondered, heal our hearts
so that our children could be healed?
So that our planet could be healed?

And what could healing possibly mean
when so much already had been lost?
When there was so much darkness?

I was soon to receive an answer to that question from the perspective of darkness. Several months after Pisti's death, a friend who had recently returned from South America came to visit us. We talked about Pisti and some of our experiences surrounding his death. Our friend suggested we go to Death Valley during the full moon and spend the night there together in meditation. We agreed. I will never forget the experience of that night.

We began our meditation in the sand dunes that evening with a ritual to honor the sacredness of all life and to call the Spirits of the four corners to be present during our work. We then took our individual places within the sacred circle and began our meditation. Hours passed, and the desert itself became alive in me—vast spaces and voluptuous dunes in the reflected light of the moon. The desert seemed to exude a pleasure that we were there. I began to feel that the landscape itself had prepared an experience for me. Only later would I discover that a large part of Death Valley forms the lowest point on the continent. This would not have interested me had I not felt myself to be at just such a low point when I began to sink beneath the desert floor.

Then there was no desert. There was no form, or, as Kerényi would say, there was only "the minimum conceivable amount of form." I was inside a neutral darkness whose energy was perfectly balanced. However, the very stability of this balance made it difficult to release myself from it. In spite of its pure potential, I had never experienced anything so oppressive. I longed for the world of light and form, but for hours I was unable to move.

Suddenly, an energy exploded out of that balance, moved through my body like an electrical current, and passed through my vocal cords in a wailing cry so filled with grief and despair that it could not form itself into words. I must have fallen briefly into unconsciousness since my next memory was of the two men holding me up and desperately splashing our drinking water onto my burning face. Only then did the energy begin to form itself into words. I was never able to remember those words, but their intention was clear: they were a lament rooted in a sorrow so deep and so intense that even the lamentation itself was shattered. Istvan was stunned into silence, but our friend responded to the voice with love and asked, "What, Great Mother, can we do to heal your pain? We are here. What can we do?" All three of us were shocked and silent as we heard the voice scream out across the desert dunes: "It can never be healed!"

From the perspective of darkness and grief I had received a living answer to my question: "What can healing mean when so many people have been destroyed by unbearable sorrow and despair?" From that perspective, healing was not possible. If the World Child had been determined to reveal to me how the consciousness of this planet had shattered its soul, he completed his mission that night.

Only gradually was I able to find words for my experience in the depths of this "underworld" or the Great Void. I knew that the mythic images for the underworld or otherworld experiences varied throughout the world depending on each culture's view of death. Some cultures associate images of torture and punishment with such a world. Other cultures associate such a world with specific characteristics that have been repressed in their conscious worldview and thus remain undeveloped in the individual before the journey to this "otherworld" occurs.

In these particular myths, a journey to the otherworld would allow the initiate to become conscious of a much larger potential within human experience. The images of such myths often reflect an experience in the deeper layers of being where mind merges with Mind and where form confronts formlessness. From the perspective of separated individual consciousness, this can be a harrowing experience, but from the perspective of Mind, this experience can provide the individual a significant insight into the essential structure of reality.

It is this essential structure of reality that is mirrored in the Greek myth of Persephone's underworld experience: it is what

Kerényi calls the "exquisite balance" of Persephone. The image of Persephone with her mother Demeter reflects the form of life, while the image of Persephone with her underworld husband reflects the minimal degree of form, which is death. Persephone was able to achieve this balance, not by seeking the realm of formlessness, but by suddenly finding herself there.

The Homeric poem tells us that she was playing in a sunlit meadow, dazzled by the beauty and fragrance of form when the earth opened and "the lord and All-receiver" sprang out of the gaping abyss and, against Persephone's will, carried her down to his dark and formless world. Persephone longed to return to her mother of light and form, and her mother, through the power of her love and grief, was able to draw her beloved daughter back to the earth again. We are told, however, that Persephone had eaten the fruit of the underworld, the pomegranate. Now she belonged to both worlds: she was bonded to life and to death, to form and to formlessness, and it was between these two polar worlds that she would create the great orbit of her "exquisite balance."

The Persephone story reflects the essential structure of the reality of every human being. That is why this mythic tale of the underworld shaped the core experience in the Mystery School at Eleusis. Just like Persephone, we too are dazzled by the beauty and fragrance of form, which we experience as life. And death, the "All-receiver" of that life, does indeed seem to spring out of the gaping abyss to take away from us all that we have ever loved. Without the Mystery, we end here—in sorrow and despair. With the Mystery, however, we experience the rest of the story: the very moment Persephone is touched by her husband of death, she conceives new life. Death impregnates Persephone. This is the secret of all the Great Mysteries: *death is the source of all life*. To experience this essential truth is to experience *The Miracle of Death*.

Indeed, an experience had been prepared for me that evening as I meditated at the lowest point on this continent in the Valley of Death. My seductive underworld husband Hades had lured me to him with the delights of desert places, seductive dunes, and the reflected light of the moon. Then, in the night, the valley floor opened and Hades sprang forth and carried me from the living into his bottomless, formless world of death. There I, the wife of Hades' formlessness and the daughter of Demeter's form, was caught in the balance of my own being. I could not move. My observing consciousness was inside the pomegranate seed of balanced vibration, a seed not yet thrusting into matter, a balance not yet expanding into form through the power of longing and love.

As wife I had eaten the seed of Hades' realm, the "fecund emptiness" of his pomegranate world, but as daughter I found his balanced realm oppressive and longed for my mother of form and flower. And so it was that this love and longing between daughter and mother broke the embrace of Hades. Filled with her husband's seed, the daughter returned, but to her sorrow, she discovered that the Great Mother was ill, and the earth was a wasteland of despair that could never be healed.

The Great Mother cried out in her agony. She asked us to hear, to know, to remember, to carry her stories in our consciousness. She was Lavinia. She was the World Child. And she was the Mother who carried their grief. Her sorrow could not be healed. But was not this sorrow itself a calling out for the awakening of the Great Bards—the visionaries, the musicians, the scientists, the actors, the poets—to chant their stories of "the immensities of the universe"? Was it not a call for us to remember our true nature of love and passion as we explode out of the heart of the cosmos? And was it not, after all, a call for each of us to awaken to our own individual work of transforming the earth's basic mentality into a planetary, multidimensional consciousness?

I had taken into myself the stories of my culture. I had listened and I had heard the stories of my life, of Lavinia, of the World Child, and of the Great Mother who carried their grief. These are the stories of the wasteland that the world must carry in its consciousness. We must carry in our hearts this sorrow that can never be healed. These are the stories of darkness, rape, and murder. Let the Great Bards chant these stories of the straight line, of beginnings and ends, of separation and despair, stories that emerge when we fail "to find our true nature," and we do not make room in ourselves for "the immensities of the universe."

And let these Bards dance with us in the Round Dance where this straight line is curved into the Great Circle of infinite possibilities. We have called the Jackal Healers to ourselves, and we are dreaming with the earth to heal our future now in this present. We will tell our children the stories of our forgetting, the stories of our darkness, the stories that collapsed the Great Round. And from this angle of our experience, we will distill our darkness into light.

A few months after our night in Death Valley, I had the following experience in "the inner space and time of consciousness."

> *I was lying on a delivery table in a hospital room filled with physicians. Pisti was one among the physicians who were preparing to perform a Caesarean section. The scene changed, and I watched Pisti lay my body in a glass coffin, which he then placed in a large oven. My consciousness was located up above my body. Slowly, I began to detect a glowing light inside my heart. As the light became more and more radiant, my body began to disappear. Finally, only the heart remained, beating and radiant.*
>
> *My consciousness then moved to the far right, which I realized was the dimension of physical time and space. I saw the jackal running to every place I had ever been on the earth and eating the dead energy forms of my life. I was elated. As the jackal ate, I felt myself giving birth. I looked back at the coffin, and saw that the heart had created a new body. With the help of the others, Pisti took my body out of the great oven. As Pisti helped me stand up, I saw that he and the others were glowing with radiant light. Pisti then placed the palms of his hands together at his heart, bowed to me, and whispered, "The Radiant One." Then each of the spirits, one by one, stood before me in the same manner and spoke in a reverent voice, "The Radiant One." Only then did I realize that my heart had given birth to a radiant, glowing body. Then I too placed the palms of my hands together at my heart and bowed to all those present and together we whispered, "A Miracle. A Miracle."*

Chapter Eight

"Dad, do you see the horizon? Even that is not the limit."

—Pisti

One morning in June of 1992 Istvan woke up and asked me if I had *The I Ching*. I did, but I wasn't sure I could find it quickly in my study. I hadn't looked at it for several years, and it had been even longer since Istvan and I had looked at it together. I asked Istvan how he had remembered the title, and he said, "I didn't. Pisti talked to me about the book and the jackal in a dream." Istvan then explained that he and Pisti had been together and that Pisti reminded Istvan that the jackal *is* a symbol for our time because he transforms the dead, the spoiled, the decayed into new life within his own system. Pisti told Istvan that the jackal is called "The Opener of the Way" because this process opens us to unlimited creativity. Istvan explained that when Pisti said the words, "Opener of the Way," the scene changed, and Istvan and Pisti were sitting on the top of a mountain overlooking the ocean. Pisti put his arm around Istvan and pointed straight ahead. "Dad," he said, "do you see the horizon? Even that is not the limit."

Then Pisti told Istvan to read the hexagram in *The I Ching* whose lines, reading from the top to the bottom, were straight, broken, broken, straight, straight, broken. "Study this hexagram carefully," Pisti said. "It is your work. It is the work of the earth." Istvan said he remembered the lines because the code is ML. "The M is made up of two straight lines and two slanting or broken lines. The L is one straight line and one fallen or broken line."

With that I jumped out of bed and ran into my study. After about ten minutes of searching, I found *The I Ching* and went back into the bedroom. Then I looked in the back pages to find the right hexagram. Reading the hexagrams from top to bottom rather than the usual way of bottom to top, I found the matching hexagram. It was number 18. I turned to the text where this hexagram was presented, but I was so startled by what I saw that I had to show Istvan rather than read it to him. We both looked at the page together:

18. Ku / Work on What Has Been Spoiled [Decay]

The Chinese character *ku* represents a bowl in whose contents worms are breeding. This means decay. It has come about because the gentle indifference of the lower trigram has come together with the rigid inertia of the upper, and the result is stagnation. Since this implies guilt, the conditions embody a demand for removal of the cause. Hence the meaning of the hexagram is not simply "what has been spoiled" but "work on what has been spoiled."

THE JUDGMENT

WORK ON WHAT HAS BEEN SPOILED

Has supreme success.
It furthers one to cross the great water.
Before the starting point, three days.
After the starting point, three days.[1]

The atmosphere in the room was electric. Pisti's consciousness could not have been more present had he been sitting in the room with us. But Pisti was not alone. Both Istvan and I felt the presence of a consciousness in the room that was composed of unique individual minds that functioned as one Mind. I began to experience the elevation of my own consciousness. Although there was no chanting, I knew I was inside the resonance of that great spiral of souls that I had experienced just after Pisti's death. I had known then, as now, that these souls were working in many dimensions to heal the earth. Many were born on the earth, took in the poisonous myth of meaninglessness, and were transforming this dead food into a living consciousness. Now they were powerfully present, here in this room, to remind us of our work. They were the Jackal Healers the earth had called. And they had chosen an ancient Chinese book of wisdom as their way to communicate with us.

This book—*The I Ching*—is based on the principles of process, change, and transformation. These principles are the *tao* of Lao-tse, "the immutable, eternal law at work in all change." According to the great German scholar of Chinese culture and translator of *The I Ching,* Richard Wilhelm, change is never meaningless because it is always subject to this universal law, the *tao.* If change were meaningless, we could have no knowledge of it. There would be no order, no regulating principle to inform us. But, according to Wilhelm, this knowledge does exist, and it is this knowledge that is presented in *The I Ching.* This ancient wisdom, which profoundly influenced Chinese culture for over three thousand years, is rooted in the worldview that Mind/Spirit is the force creating the visible world. Since the human being is a manifestation of this force, each person's thoughts, feelings, and choices play a role in the changes and transformations of our planet.[2]

I asked Istvan about the code ML. "Why," I wondered, "was the hexagram presented in this way?" Istvan responded that these letters were chosen because they not only identify the hexagram but they describe the Jackal Healers. Pisti had explained to Istvan that the Jackal Healers are *Merchants of Light* because *they are able to distill darkness into light,* and, like merchants, they "sell" the knowledge of this process for the "price" of consciousness, and the entire universe "profits." This process releases a resonance on the earth that brings about what we call *miracles;* therefore, they are also known as Miracle Lovers. Since all of their work is done in harmony with the deep Matrix of

Life, the mother source, they are Mother Love. And since they work on multidimensional levels of life, they live Multi-Lives on Multi-Levels. They carry the Memory of Light; thus they are Masters of Light, Masters of Love and Masters of Life.

Istvan said that as soon as he had understood the code in the dream, Pisti laughed and jokingly said, "Tell your 'mother' that they could be called 'Jackal Bodhisattvas' except that they do not *reject* 'nirvana.' In the universe there is only *Now*; therefore, their essence is always in nirvana 'at the same time' that they are creating many lives on many levels. Those lives always include their work as healers in worlds that call them." Istvan then looked at me and said, "Well, Kicsi, that was for you. I felt Pisti wanted to answer some question you had in your mind when I was telling you about ML in the dream—even though, in this reality, I had to wake up to tell you. Maybe he was trying to help me see how everything really is happening at once."

We both laughed at how Pisti related to each of us in a different way. It was true that Istvan was not really interested in bodhisattvas and nirvana. He had experienced the essence of ML and had no desire for further explanations, yet I wanted to understand ML in relation to such experiences in other cultures. Suddenly Istvan turned to me and said, "But that's your work, Kicsi. You are the one who always stays to write about ML." Only later would I understand the painful meaning of this statement.

For now, however, I needed to focus on Istvan's experience. Its significance for us and for the earth was so immense that it took time for my brain to grasp it. Finally, I said to Istvan, "If our work and the work of the earth is to become the Jackal Healers we have called, then this code of ML is the code of our own transformation." Istvan said, "Yes, that's what Pisti meant when he told you that the earth would be healed because we had called our future to ourselves. They are our future." Then he added, "But there is a lot of work to be done."

As I thought about this work, I remembered a dream I had had several months earlier. My perspective was from outer space so that I could see the sphere of the earth. As I moved closer, I saw a huge cauldron at the North Pole. Gradually I realized that Pisti was there as a jackal man with other jackal men. Together they were stirring the contents of the cauldron and working feverishly to keep them in the cauldron so they would not spill out and cover the earth. Pisti looked at me and said, "The time is critical." I asked Pisti what was in the cauldron, and all the jackals answered at once, "Shit. Unclaimed shit." They were serious and yet jovial. I understood very well that the work of each of us was to claim our own "shit" from the cauldron. Had we acknowledged our own darkness on a daily basis, it would not have been forced into the collective cauldron that now threatened the life of the planet. We were being called to distill our darkness into light. Our experiences, Istvan's and mine, had not only confirmed the urgency of this work but they also had confirmed the work's powerful transformative potential.

Later I carefully read the hexagram again along with the commentaries. I was a little disturbed when I read Wilhelm's statement that "the images on which the hexagrams are based serve as patterns for timely action in the situations indicated."[3] I thought about "timely action" and remembered that knowing precisely the right moment to dig up the decayed food was an integral aspect of the jackal symbolism. The jackal knew, states Robert Lawlor, that if the right moment was lost, the food would move into "an indigestible, untransmuted state of disassociation or chaos; then the possibility of a cyclic rebirth in a continuity from death to new life could be lost."[4]

As I continued to study Wilhelm's commentaries and his stress on "the right moment," I became more and more disturbed. The individual, he insisted, plays an important role in the outcome of world events. The earlier we are able to recognize a problem in its "germinal phase," the greater influence we can have on its outcome. "The germinal phase is the crux. As long as things are in their beginnings they can be controlled, but once they have grown to their full consequences they acquire a power so overwhelming that man stands impotent before them."[5]

Logically, it seemed to me that the situation on the earth had long passed its "germinal phase," yet the dreams and visions insisted that *Now* was the time for action. And when I read that "The Judgment" in *The I Ching* was always a reflection of the quality of the moment in which one receives the hexagram, I realized that *The I Ching* was also in agreement that the "critical time" is *Now*: "WORK ON WHAT HAS BEEN SPOILED/ Has supreme success./ It furthers one to cross the great water."

We have abused our human freedom, according to *The I Ching*, by our "gentle indifference" and "rigid inertia." It is we who have fostered decay and stagnation. How can such a terrible condition be transformed? The answer from *The I Ching* is this: only if we replace indifference and inertia with "decisiveness" and "energy." Success depends on our willingness not to "recoil from work and danger." It also depends on "proper deliberation," our ability to evaluate each phase of our work. *The I Ching* states that,

> *We must first know the causes of corruption before we can do away with them; hence it is necessary to be cautious during the time before the start. Then we must see to it that the new way is safely entered upon, so that a relapse may be avoided; therefore we must pay attention to the time after the start.*[6]

I felt that most of my adult life had been a "deliberation" on the "causes of corruption." I knew that the very nature of human existence provides us with the freedom to forget the principles of creativity, to become "indifferent," and to sink into "rigid inertia." It is always an abuse of our freedom to take life for granted, forget that "we can do nothing but create," and fall by default, *deus absconditus*, to the bottom of the barrel where we suffer inside the anti-myth of meaninglessness, chance, addiction, fragmentation, and violence.

I was moved by the fact that the first five lines in the hexagram, moving from the bottom to the top, are about working on what has been spoiled either by the father or the mother, the "parents," that is, our culture. It is, says Wilhelm, a "corruption originating from neglect in former times" and is therefore a call to work on "inner conditions."[7] We could just as easily say that this hexagram is a call to participate in the "desperately and urgently required project for our time—to explore the inner space and time of consciousness" before the consequences of inaction "acquire a power so overwhelming" that we will stand impotent before them.

Wilhelm emphasizes that this work can be accomplished only if love prevails and extends over both the beginning and the end.[8] This seemed appropriate to me since we surely need compassion and understanding for ourselves and others when we work with a darkness that has the power to destroy us. When Istvan and I talked about this, he said that the root of all the ML symbolism is "Sira," Matrix Love, the powerful and pervasive love at the heart of the cosmos. "Everything, the whole universe, has its source in her heart." Then he said, "I say 'her' heart, but actually 'she' is beyond gender. Maybe I should say she is androgynous."

I found it interesting that the Egyptian symbolism of the jackal had merged with the Chinese symbolism in *The I Ching*. I had known very little about these two symbolic systems before they appeared in our dreams and visions. Both systems were in harmony with the same great *tao* that organizes all life. It seemed to me that the merging of these two systems within our lives was symbolic of the *worldwide* urgency of working on what has corrupted culture and is now threatening life as we know it on this planet.

I thought about the practical and functional quality of the jackal symbolism. Evidently, my dreaming mind had not been able to find a symbol in my Western mythic tradition that could reflect the necessary work of our time as well as does the Egyptian jackal. His animal nature of instinct, flesh, and process could evoke my own instinctual knowledge of matter, the body, and the process of decomposition and transformation. Judaeo-Christian culture had become too consciously refined and distanced from the body and the older levels of the brain to provide the necessary symbols for integrating many of these excluded realities. In Christianity, for example, the images of the divine were restricted to a masculine human trinity. The plethora of images from the female body, from animals, and, in fact, from all nature were deplored as "fallen matter." Fallen matter not only lacked divinity but reflected its opposite—"evil." Such an attitude, supported in earlier centuries by the powers of both Church and State, had long paralyzed our creative use of symbolic language.

Another reason for the distancing and neglect of the body and the older levels of the brain has been our emphasis on conceptual thinking, the word and the written text. Gradually we lost our intuitive knowledge of the need for images in brain functioning. However, modern research in brain development can now help us remember why the brain needs images. In the words of Lawlor, "Each new brain structure grew as a peripheral envelope encasing the older brain component. Beneath the cerebral cortex the two earlier forms are still performing as they did in our most remote ancestors."[9] *Therefore, we need a language that can communicate with and activate all of the various components.*

Carl Sagan once said that "the hallmark of a successful, long-lived civilization may be the ability to achieve a lasting peace among the several brain components."[10] Schwaller de Lubicz understood this necessity. He knew, states Lawlor, that all ancient cultures that were grounded in the symbolic method were

> *educating the neurological structure of the brain to maintain an active, conscious connection not only between the bilateral lobes of the cerebral cortex, but also with the impulses and subliminal information received from the ancient and deeper limbic and reptilian centers, so that these aspects of our nature could be integrated into the activity of our reasoning mind.*[11]

In the West we have denigrated our animal nature and thus failed to realize that it offers us "a vast instinctual intelligence of the laws of nature."[12]

When I found myself wondering if I were really capable of dissolving the old limitations of my cultural thinking, I remembered the jackal, that part of me which carried the vital knowledge of dissolution and rebirth. He reminded me that my own ancient brain and body knew how to bring about radical transformation. From his first appearance in my dream, he had reflected his animal nature as the jackal, but he was a jackal in a deep state of meditation. Then, as he promised me that he could give me a knowledge beyond books, he transformed himself into living darkness and announced that he was "the All, the Void." In this one dream, the jackal symbolism demonstrated its ability to connect instinctual knowledge to the highest divine principle of Oneness. This was exciting. I now needed to know if such a series of interconnected jackal images existed in Egyptian mythology. I was in for some astounding surprises.

From Arthur Versluis' *The Egyptian Mysteries* I learned that Anubis is a multifaceted symbol of the *bridge* between the least developed and most developed states of being. He is Hermanubis, both Hermes and Anubis, the guide of souls into the Great Mysteries. He connects the dark nonmanifest world of Nephthys to the light manifest world of Isis as he circles through the below and into the above. Since Anubis himself is that circular movement that connects these realms, he is called the "Horizon" that is visible to both.[13]

The fact that Hermanubis is connected to the oldest levels of brain development makes him accessible to everyone, even those "in the most infernal mental states." He awakens in us the watchfulness of the dog who is able to see as well in the dark as in the light and who is able to discern between friend and foe, illusion and reality. He is Thoth (that part of the mind capable of memory and reflection), the scribe who records what Hermanubis reveals. Anubis is black and gold, dark and light, below and above. From him we receive the "scent of the Divine" that guides us into the knowledge of Osiris—the Mystery itself.[14]

I marveled at the emergence of these forms into my own consciousness. This emergence reflected a cognition that remembered more than I individually knew. The jackal imagery in my dream had followed the same principles of organization as the Egyptian jackal imagery. The pattern created by that organization was not only a bridge between the oldest and newest brain components but a circular, continuous *movement* that opens up and activates our unlimited creative capacities. The excitement reached its peak with this image of the dynamic flow of energy in healthy brain functioning. The mind, in my dream and in the Egyptian myth, had reflected back to itself an image of how it functions in a state of health and wholeness.

This image helped me to comprehend the violent and destructive consequences of a worldview that excludes and represses significant aspects of the mind. It also gave another dimension to my dream of world catastrophe. In this dream the mind reflected the devastating *planetary* consequences of this worldview. We had raped our heart and the heart of the world by denying our wholeness. And once again the mind presented the blueprint for its own healing: the circular flow of energy in the Round Dance. As each individual in the dream began to dance, a powerful momentum was created throughout the entire planet. This was a beautiful image of individuals healing together and creating a new planetary consciousness. Hermanubis is the "Round Dance" that heals the "raped heart."

As I thought about how Hermanubis and the hexagram from *The I Ching* reflect the necessary work of our time, I remembered a statement from Carl Jung: "One does not become enlightened by imagining figures of light, but by making the darkness conscious." This wisdom had existed for centuries in the underground tradition of Western culture, but the dominant tradition tended to reduce life into opposing forces of evil and good. Rather than focusing on the *process* of consciously transforming the darkness we all carry, the focus was on figures of light in whom there is "no darkness at all."[15]

The underground alchemists attempted to compensate for this dangerously unbalanced attitude by emphasizing that the great work for all of us begins with the claiming and transforming of our own personal darkness. Their actual reference to this darkness as "excrement" reflects their effort to refocus our attention from "figures of light" to those aspects of ourselves that we dislike, deny, reject, and repress. It is inside this darkness that our work begins, and only from this darkness can we distill the light.

This is the work that "opens the way" to the unlimited creativity of multidimensional Mind. As we become skilled in the continuous process of transforming our own personal, familial, and cultural darkness into light, we become the "Masters of Light" we have called to ourselves. We know ourselves as immanental Mind and we experience ourselves as the creative energy that is moving us toward a "new planetary culture." We *are* the earth dreaming a dream to heal herself, and, slowly and carefully, we are beginning to dream together the sacred steps of the Round Dance.

Chapter Nine

"Death is as Divine as Life.
Hold them in both hands, Kicsi.
Play with them.
Balance them.
This is the Divine Game."

—Istvan

Two years had passed since Pisti's death. Istvan and I had bought a beautiful piece of land—a little "woods"—with a creek running through it. I planned to take an early retirement from teaching so I would have time to write. Istvan would continue his business on a reduced scale, but he would still have some of his equipment made in Hungary so he could visit his family and friends once a year. We were excited about this new possibility of living a simple life in nature.

In the meantime, one of our nephews from Hungary, Tibor, came to live with us so that he could study English. He spent the weekdays with us and the weekends with Istvan's brother and his wife, Paul and Adel. Tibi's presence ignited Istvan's old spirit of play: together they went golfing, bowling, and to the horse races. When I told them that I was happy to see them having such a good time but was a little concerned that I had not heard one word of English pass between them, they both laughed and insisted that five mornings of school each week was quite enough to give to English.

Istvan and I took the weekends to continue our inner work—to meditate, listen to music, read, and talk. We were often with Jenny during these times, and together we talked about the profound significance and interconnectedness of our combined experiences. Istvan and I hoped and believed that Jenny was beginning to open herself up to life again. Each of us knew that our experiences were a sacred trust—one that required our transformation, a new worldview, and a radically creative life.

In the midst of our planning for this new way of life and less than two weeks before Tibi arrived, I had the following dream on October 30, 1993:

> *I am in Spain. Some friends and I have been shopping, and we return with a few beautiful objects that we have purchased. We do not return to a hotel, but to a large, magnificent cathedral. We walk up the stairs and a tall door is opened for us. As I enter, the atmosphere of the dream shifts from playfulness to profound sacredness. I realize that this cathedral is the living center of the political and social world and that its power flows from its roots in the world of nonphysical reality. A ritual of great importance is in process. I understand the significance of this ritual at once. I give everything I am holding to the person who has opened the door for us. Then I see that the cathedral has no roof; it is open to the sky.*
>
> *Directly in front of me are stairs that go down deep into darkness. I realize that I am dressed completely in black. I move to my left and begin the descent. I know that I am entering a very different energy field. With each step I take downward, I feel the energy permeate me and synchronize my system with its own. I know I am prepared for whatever I must experience. To my upper right, however, near the top of the stairs, I see two or three of the women with whom I entered. They are quietly and somewhat aimlessly dancing on the upper steps in what I feel is their attempt to ignore the necessity to descend the stairs.*
>
> *As I continue to descend, I look to my right. I realize that I am looking at the very source of this strange and powerful ritual. At the center of a large rectangle that is located in the floor at the center of the cathedral is a Shiva-like figure with many arms and legs. I realize that this figure is the center of all being, of all that has ever been, of all that will ever be. He/she is seated in a yoga position, and yet the arms and legs are dancing an*

exquisite dance. All the hands are holding large black ostrich feathers whose delicate, artistic movement is part of the dance. The entire body is dark and is covered with a transparent, black material that fits like skin. Draped over the shoulders is a beautiful black robe that forms a perfect circle around the figure.

Forming another circle around this figure are several similar figures. They are not seated; they are lying on their backs while their numerous arms and legs dance in complete harmony with the dance of the central figure. Their dance also includes the delicate movement of the black ostrich feathers. I feel the power, the energy, the sacredness of this ritual. As I continue to descend, I see the head of the central figure move backward and the mouth open wide. I see darkness in the mouth, and I hear the deep sounds of the word V-O-I-D as it slowly flows out of the throat and fills the entire cathedral.

When I awoke the next morning, Istvan had already left for work. I met my friend Maria for our usual morning walk. She and I always discussed our dreams as we walked the trail. Over the years we had discussed many dreams and many phases of our lives. Both of us had always been very intense in our determination to understand the human mind, and this had led to her becoming a therapist and to my continued study of symbolic, mythic language.

Of course, this morning I told her my dream. As I talked, I struggled to release myself from its ominous and awesome grip. I remember saying, "I wonder what life has in store for me now. My only other dream of the Void came just a few months before Pisti's death." We noted how the person I identified with was immediately willing to descend the stairs, but the other women, obviously parts of myself, were not. At the time, I felt these other women, in spite of their reluctance, eventually would have to participate in the ritual of descent, but later I would see them as parts of my consciousness that would keep me anchored in the world of time and space.

About four months later, early in the morning of March 3, 1994, the doorbell rang. Istvan was in Hungary, so I got up to go to the door. I saw that Tibi's door was closed, so I knew he was asleep. I went first into Istvan's office in the front of the house so I could look out the window to see who was ringing the bell at this early hour. I saw Istvan's brother, Paul, and his wife, Adel. I ran to the door and opened it. Then everything happened very quickly. I asked, "What has happened? Has there been an accident?" Paul answered, "Yes." I felt my hands come together at my heart as if in prayer and I heard myself say, "Please don't tell me it is Istvan. Don't tell me it is Istvan too." I saw Paul's lips say "Yes." I heard myself ask, "Is he dead?" and again I saw Paul's lips say "Yes."

I felt and heard myself screaming, "No, not Istvan too. I can't live on the earth without Istvan too. Not Istvan too." I later realized that I must have tried to run away because Paul and Adel were holding me securely in one spot. I don't know how long I screamed or when I seated myself on the couch. I don't remember Adel covering my shoulders with a blanket. I only remember that, after what seemed a very long time, my mind returned from a vast space of darkness. I felt energy moving from my left hand into my heart. I looked over to see that Paul was holding my hand, and I said, "I have to go to Hungary today," and he said, "Yes." Then I asked, "Will you go with me?" and he said, "Yes."

Friends began to arrive and to call. All morning we grieved together as I packed and they helped me make the arrangements to fly to Budapest that afternoon. I heard Maria say to Adel to make a reservation for her too. This was an unexpected gift of the heart. I knew she would be an anchor for me in the world of spirit. By noon Paul, Tibi, Maria, and I embarked on a journey that would mark my descent through the mouth of Shiva into the heart of the Void.

During the flight to Budapest, I closed my eyes and tried to allow myself to experience the essence of Istvan's death. My own personal grief was so profound that there were moments when I feared that I might be overwhelmed by it. During these moments I breathed deeply and prayed that I could carry this grief with inner dignity. For me, this meant allowing myself consciousness of my own sorrow without it splashing out on others. I felt I would be able to do this if I could grasp the larger significance of Istvan's death.

At first, I could only think about practical details. Was anyone else involved in the accident? Was anyone else killed? How did the accident actually occur? This time I was the one who would go to the scene of the accident, see the car, talk to the police, handle the necessary details. My brother had done this when my mother was killed. Istvan had done this when Pisti died. I had not wanted to see where Mother died. It had been difficult enough to imagine my mother crossing the road and suddenly becoming aware of a car that, only seconds later, would hit her and throw her over the car and into a ditch. Nor had I wanted to see Pisti's mangled car, his music tapes strewn out across the freeway. But this time it would be different. Now it was my turn.

I thought of Istvan's body. Would it be crushed? Would I choose to see it? This beautiful world of matter—in such moments we experience how much we love the physical form. I felt an unbearable sorrow for the loss of form. I felt my own body scream out in the interior silence of its loss, "Why, Istvan, why did you have to go too?" It was in that moment that I felt Istvan's presence for the first time. "Kicsi, I didn't *go* anywhere. I'm right here, everywhere, and nowhere. I'm simply in another dimension. Let the body go. I'm not in that body. I don't need it anymore."

There was such a feeling of joy in Istvan's words that my own emotions shifted abruptly. From the center of my head I felt a double shaft of light merge and flood through my body to the core of the earth. Now I could understand Istvan's vision of how he and Pisti create together—sometimes as one person and sometimes as two people—like twins. That twin energy had now merged and a celebration was taking place. From within my own body, I looked up and realized that I had become a century plant that was bursting into blossom high in the sky. Beautiful birds were fluttering around the flowers in great delight. My own heart exploded in joy. Shiva had swallowed: I was *in* the heart of the Void.

Of course, I was also in a culture that would deem me mad if I allowed myself to rave about twins, century plants, and the Void. And I was in a body that longed for the physical forms of those I loved. But at least I knew that it was possible to experience simultaneously the presence of spirit and the absence of form.

When I arrived in Hungary, I went to the place where Istvan died. Two of Istvan's brothers, Paul and Tibor, Tibi's father, Maria and I went there together. Tibor had talked earlier with the police and had some of the details of the accident. Istvan had been speeding and had swerved off the road. The road was level with a wide strip of flat land, so he could have driven back onto the road with no difficulty had he not left the road precisely at a spot where there was a small tree stump. His car hit the stump, was thrown into the air and landed on the ground with such a force that Istvan was thrown out of the car. The car then bounced into the air once again and fell on Istvan's head.

The police had removed the car except for a bumper that was lying in the grass. I saw the stump. Then I went to the spot where Istvan died. There was an indentation in the earth where his head had been. Now, only his blood remained. All around tiny blue spring flowers were growing close to the earth. As I picked some of them, I noticed their beautiful gold center. I placed them on the bloodstained earth. As I returned to our car, I noticed that Maria had placed flowers on the stump. From there we went to the police station. I looked at the mangled car. I saw Istvan's blood, skin, and hair on the broken glass.

As I looked at these violently scattered fragments of Istvan's body, the dream of my descent into the Void just four months earlier strengthened me. I knew now that the sacred ritual in which I had participated was the Mystery of Death. Istvan's death. In the dream I had felt prepared for whatever I was to experience. And I felt strangely prepared now.

Just as in the dream, I had been called to release everything so that I could enter the "underworld"—once again—on its terms. I noted that this dream was very different from the ones before Pisti's accident in which the knowledge of his death repeatedly attempted to penetrate my consciousness, but I simply could not accept it. I was not able to identify with the mother in the dream who could accept her son's death. While this last dream did not reveal specifically that it was Istvan's death that I was to experience, it was clear that I would be required to enter into the Void and to submit myself to the principle of dissolution. The major character in the dream immediately understood the significance of the ritual, released everything, and submitted herself to the laws of the underworld—*and I had identified with that character.* A major shift in my basic mentality actually had taken place.

Still the grief was present. I accepted it. I even welcomed it as a gift from the underworld, for it was the threads of grief that allowed me to weave a different kind of consciousness. A Mayan oracle states that "Polarity is the loom on which reality is strung." Now I could understand that to be alive is to be this loom, and to weave the fabric of life we need the threads of birth and death, light and dark, joy and sorrow. I was now able to hold the threads of death in one hand and the threads of life in the other. Whether I felt sorrow or joy, both were always present. I was learning to play with both of them. I was learning to balance them. I was learning to play the "Divine Game."

Holding the threads of these powerful opposites meant allowing myself to experience each at deep levels. Only later would I realize that I had such a conscious determination to maintain my balance and to appreciate all the gifts in my life that it had to be my body and my dreaming self that kept the balance on the side of sorrow. My rational mind was well aware that there were gifts within the tragedies: my mother, Pisti, and Istvan had quick deaths and did not have to live in severely damaged bodies. Mother died first and did not have to experience Pisti's and Istvan's deaths and my sorrow. Istvan was with me during Pisti's death. Both Istvan and I had experienced the continuous creativity of Mind. I had good friends who were loving and present, and I had a supportive community. Almost every day I heard stories of people who had suffered enormous losses within circumstances that made healing almost impossible. My rational mind *obliged* me to heal.

But it was my body and my dreaming, symbolic mind that *allowed* me to heal. My body held within its very molecular structure the memory of every event and the dates of every nuance of sorrow. The intelligence of my body regulated the rhythms and cycles of my grieving and healing. While I was able to walk through each day in gratitude for the gifts of my life, it was my body that pulled me back into the silence of aloneness, grief, and healing.

And my body spoke to me in its ancient symbolic language. I felt as though the wise "Elders" of the Imagination sat in a circle around me, each in a state of meditation, each synchronized with the body, mind, and heart of the soul they held in their inner vision. I imagined them releasing images, synchronizing events, and speaking through my body's weaknesses and pains. Had it not been for the dream images, the waking visions, and the images that seemed to arise out of the body itself, I could not have experienced healing.

Later I would remember a quotation from Jung that accurately expressed my feeling at that time.

> *To the extent that I managed to translate the emotions into images – that is to say, to find the images which were concealed in the emotions – I was inwardly calmed and reassured. Had I left those images hidden in the emotions, I might have been torn to pieces by them.*[1]

The Elders themselves, of course, were just such images "concealed," if not in my emotions or my body, then in the organizing principles of my Imagination. Like "transformers" they took multidimensional consciousness and stepped it down to an image-currency that I could receive and integrate into my daily life. I too was aware that I stood between the two possibilities of either being "torn to pieces" by my emotions or being "calmed and reassured" by the images.

Several months, maybe even a year, after Istvan's death, I had the following dream. It was so painful that I did not record it, and, therefore, I do not have the date.

> *There has been a terrible accident. Someone comes to tell me, and I rush to the place where it has occurred. No one seems to know the identity of the dead person. The people standing around are preoccupied with something else, but I am down on my hands and knees with a transparent glass bowl. I am gathering the scattered pieces of the body and placing them carefully into the bowl. When all the pieces have been collected, I sit down in the street. Alone now, I embrace the bowl and hold it in my lap. I begin to emit a wailing sound that finally shapes itself into the words, "This is the body of* my *child."*

Through these images this avalanche of grief for both Pisti and Istvan could be released without restraint. In the dream I was the mother, but I was also a conscious observer who was viewing the dream as a film. Through the dream's distancing of me to the position of observer, I was allowed to experience my grieving self as *the woman* holding the pieces of her child's dead body.

In stark contrast to the woman were the people who did not know the identity of the dead person and were preoccupied with something else. I felt that these people were aspects of myself. They were present but were not allowing themselves to be fully conscious of the event. They seemed to reflect my preoccupation with survival and my "obligation" to heal.

Yet the person with whom I identified in the dream allowed herself to sink to the bottom of her grief. She embraced death as she held the transparent tomb in her lap. From the perspective of matter, she has experienced a total loss. Never will she experience her child in the physical world again. This is the reality she *must* grieve.

This dream reflected how my psyche had divided the labor of survival *and* healing within itself. I could see that both aspects were necessary. I needed those parts of myself that focused on reconstructing my life and on evaluating my sorrow within the framework of the enormous suffering in the world. Yet I also had to allow myself to experience the depth of my own grief. As I reflected on the intelligence of this process taking place within me, I was, indeed, calmed and reassured.

There was yet another dream—one from long ago—that now reassured me of the timeless intelligence of Mind. I had had the dream on November 25, 1989, before the deaths of Mother, Pisti, or Istvan. That dream had always puzzled me, but since their deaths I was able to look at it from another perspective. Now I could see that in this dream I had been allowed once again to step through a window into the future, even though I would not be able to understand my experience until that future arrived.

> *I am in a two-story house that is being built in the desert. Only the frame exists. I am in a bedroom upstairs, but I cannot go to sleep because there is a sinister creature crouching in the dark. He is both human and animal. I know he is ready to spring forward and, like a primeval force, destroy me utterly. His essence pervades the room with cold emptiness, negation and death. I am frightened to the core of my being, but I keep a steady eye on him. Then, like a streak of lightning, he strikes. In the next scene I am standing at the window spitting out pieces of his heart and liver.*
>
> *Then I walk toward the frame of a door that leads into another room. I see a very large white owl standing in the doorway. I know I must pass this owl and enter the room. Once I enter the room, I am in the center of a circle of women. I have a small red box in my hands that contains the jewels of my life. I open it, step before each woman in the circle and allow her to select a jewel from the box. I understand that everyone I love must be released to death. In the deepest grief of my life, I step back into the center of the circle.*
>
> *As I start to close the lid to the empty box, I see that a rose quartz stone has miraculously appeared there. I know this is a symbol for the heart. Suddenly, I turn to my left and look beyond the circle into another dimension where I see Pisti and Istvan waiting for me. I then realize that I have been on a long journey.*

Now I remembered the profound sorrow I had experienced in that 1989 dream. It was the same sorrow I now felt. In the notes that I had written at the time of the dream, I stated, "To give away the jewels was to lose Pisti and Istvan." I had tried to interpret this part of the dream symbolically but had not been successful. How remarkable, I thought, that I had mourned the deaths of Mother, Pisti, and Istvan *before* they actually occurred. In spite of the fact that I had already discovered that I had mourned Pisti's death in dreams before he died, I realized once again that the soul can grieve for future realities.

Yet this particular dream was remarkable in another way as well since it reflected my life struggle with the Western myth of materialism. In the first scene I was totally focused on "a sinister creature," which I experienced as "a primeval force" that had the power to destroy me. The essence of this force was cold emptiness, negation, and death. Fear pervaded the core of my being, for I knew that *this* was the force that shatters the soul.

The manner in which this creature crouched in the dark corner ever ready to destroy the fabric of life was a true reflection of the horrible power this myth had in my life and in the life of my culture. It would not be for several years in the future that I would be able to spit out the last major pieces of the body of this poisonous myth. However, at the time of the dream, this power was still alive in me. Yet, *in the dream*, I consumed *it* and spat out the pieces of its dead body.

I felt the nucleus of this dream to be the woman standing in the center of a circle of women. She had reached this center by her victory over cold materialism. The first room in the dream was filled with fear, meaningless death, and fruitless emptiness. The entrance to the second room was guarded by the white owl of death and wisdom, a bird who sees through the darkness. This room was filled with grief, but this grief was experienced within the context of meaning and rebirth.

The woman experienced the death of everyone she loved as she stepped out of the center of the circle and allowed each of the women to choose a jewel from her container of life. As she grieved, she herself was "contained" by the circle of women who now held the life force of all that she loved. As the woman stepped back into the center of the circle, she entered into that "essential structure of the universe" where all extremes are exquisitely "balanced against one another," and out of her *emptiness*, she experienced a miraculous birth of the heart.

These were the powerful dreams that were shaping me for the future, but there were others, more direct and less symbolic, that I had had within the last months of Istvan's life. In one dream, on December 27, 1993, I called out to my brother and then put my hand over my mouth in astonishment and said, "Oh, my God, I called to you in the name of my dead husband."

In the fall of 1993, I dreamed that Istvan told me that he was leaving me. I felt as though he was simply leaving *me*, but I knew that he was going to die. I told him I understood, but I felt completely abandoned, and I grieved so deeply that I did not want to go on living.

Neither Istvan nor I looked at the dreams literally. This no longer surprises me since I understand now that the mind balances its knowing with its not knowing for the sake of its own well being. I told Istvan that I thought the dreams reflected my fear that he too might die. That interpretation seemed reasonable to both of us, and more than once Istvan said, "Kicsi, I wouldn't want you to experience my death too, but don't worry. I'm not going to die."

Yet Istvan himself began having powerful experiences of his death four months after Pisti died. Of course, we discussed the possibility that these dreams and visions might be reflecting his actual physical death, but Istvan rejected this view. In the beginning he felt they reflected the transformation that was taking place within him. Later, he wasn't so sure why he continued to have what felt like constant reminders that he was going to die. Even so, he never accepted that they were precognitions of his actual death.

Istvan's first dream experience of his death was so real and so terrifying that, when the experience was over, he could hardly believe he was still alive. I woke up one morning to see Istvan looking at me as though he could not believe he was actually seeing me. I sat up immediately and asked him what was wrong. "I died. Kicsi, I was dead. Gone. No tomorrow. It was all over. Nothing could be done to save me." He looked around the room and then back to me. "Kicsi, I am back from the dead."

Then he told me what he had experienced. This was on March 16, 1992:

> *I was lying on the bed when, suddenly, I saw Pisti's left arm move toward me and grab my hand. Just as I saw the black panther flash on his wrist, I was aware of an explosion. I wondered if the furnace had blown up or if there had been an earthquake. There was blood everywhere. Then I was being carried on a stretcher to an ambulance that was in front of our house. I couldn't see you, but I knew you were running by my side. I saw my brother Paul running in front of me toward the ambulance. Little Paulcsi was also there just looking around, not knowing quite what was happening. Then I heard a voice say, "It's over. You can go to the hospital if you want to, but there is nothing that anyone can do for you. Nothing. You are dead."*

Istvan insisted that this experience was symbolic, as well as those that followed. But one morning Istvan said, "I experience dying so often that I don't even want to close my eyes anymore." Of course, I asked him again if he felt there was even a suggestion of his physical death. And again, he responded, "No, I don't get that feeling. I just think there's something I need to learn, but I'm not sure what it is. I just want to live and love, but the truth is, Kicsi, that these experiences are scaring the shit out of me."

That morning we talked a long time about the experiences and just what it might be that "death" was trying to teach him. Finally, Istvan said, "What I need to learn may be clearer than I thought. If the experiences are scaring the shit out of me, then maybe the problem is my fear of death." This seemed reasonable to both of us. Istvan said that his fear of death was not a fear that death was the end of everything. Nor was it a fear of the actual death process. What he feared was the end of his individual life as Istvan here in this time and this place. Istvan loved life more than anyone I had ever known. Now that he had awakened to the loving consciousness in the universe, he felt there was so much he could do here. Finally, near the end of our discussion, he said, "Maybe what I need to learn from all this is that everything will be just as it is intended to be, just as it needs to be. I think I just need to trust this."

Then on September 19, 1992, Istvan had another experience of death. In this experience his fear and his resistance were laid bare before him. He knew he was going to die, and he fought it with all the energy that was within him. Suddenly he became aware that Pisti was present when Pisti handed him a sword. When Istvan asked him what the sword was all about, Pisti smiled and Istvan immediately understood the humor in his battle against the very process of life itself.

Yet Istvan's fear remained. As his fear increased, he was engulfed in darkness and chaos. He felt afraid that he was going to die, that I would be left alone, and that he would not be able to complete his life. Then he felt Pisti's finger on his back. A loving warmth began to flow into him through that one small spot:

> *This helped to ground me. So I just gritted my teeth and waited for death. When I didn't die, I thought, "Oh, thank God, it's over. I'm not going to die." And then, boom! I knew I* was *going to die. Then I thought, "Oh my God, it's* not *over. I'm not out of the woods yet."*
>
> *I heard Pisti's voice, "Flow with the force. Relax and let yourself flow with it." Then somehow I started to loosen up a bit. I focused on the warm spot on my back. As I felt that warm energy flow through my body, I was able to relax. Then I realized that my energy and the flow were the same.*
>
> *I knew that my own fear had hardened me and solidified me and thrown me out of the flow. That's when the darkness and chaos came. My fear had separated me from my own energy and from the energy of the life force. I was fighting against myself. It was wasted energy. This force did not need to be fought or tested or proven. It just needed to be experienced.*

It was like the experience you had with Pisti when you and he were surfing on the ocean of life. When you doubted or feared or wanted to hold onto a particular moment, you became heavy and started to sink. Well, when I was afraid that I was going to die, I became as hard as steel, and I couldn't even feel the power of the flow. I just wanted the moment of my life as Istvan "to linger."

However, as long as I kept my focus on that warm spot on my back, I felt good, and I didn't fear anything. That cleared my mind, and I started to experience the power that was in the flow. It wasn't the kind of power you can possess, but you can flow with it and create with it.

*Suddenly, I thought, "My God, I'm experiencing '*the *force of pure creativity.'" I was totally relaxed. I knew that the "essence" of the whole thing is forever, so there is no perishing of anything. I started to laugh like hell when I remembered how Pisti had given me a sword to fight it when all I had to do was flow with it and create out of it.*

"Did you die?" I asked. "Well, Kicsi, that's not such an easy question anymore. I did and I didn't. From the perspective of the flow, there doesn't seem to be any real division between what we call life and death. I guess I did die because I saw myself hang my body on a hanger just like it was an old coat. Pisti and I had a good laugh when we saw the jaw hanging open. But later I slipped back into it, and then Pisti said, 'Dad, you don't need to fear death. You have done it many times.'"

"Then," I asked, "are you still afraid of death?" And Istvan said, "Well, Kicsi, that's also not so easy to answer because I don't want to die. I simply don't want my life in this body to end. So I guess I have to say that I am afraid of dying because, flow or no flow, I simply do not want to die—and that's all there is to it."

So the issue remained unresolved. Istvan struggled with the recurring dreams and visions of his death, but he continued to insist that they were symbolic, not precognitive. At the same time, we were experiencing the wonder and joy in the universe in other dreams and visions. This made it easier to push the death motif to the side. Then on November 10, 1993, the second year anniversary of Pisti's death, Istvan had yet another death experience. He was lying in our meditation room listening to music when he felt the presence of the Great Mother. She brought the consciousness that he was going to die soon. He argued with her. He told her he loved her, but that he refused to die. But, Istvan said, something just kept telling him,

> *"You are going to die. You are dying. This is it." And I said, "No, I'm not. You can do whatever else you want with me, but I refuse to die." And I mean we fought. I tracked the time. One side of the tape finished and the other side was half through before our argument let up. I just told her that I did not care what she wanted, I was not going to die. But then she said, "You are going to die anyway. Remember. It is time. It is your choice. Everything is right on schedule."*
>
> *And I just kept repeating, "I am not going to die." Then I announced that I was going to get up to pee. "Well," she said, "that's good. That's a good check with reality for you." Then I said, "Fine, I'll hold it. I don't give a damn. I'm still not going to die." Well, eventually, I got up and peed anyway. It was a struggle, Kicsi, a hell of a struggle. This fighting with death is getting boring. I seemed to know that this fight was a waste of time, but I was compelled to do it anyway.*

As I now listened to the recording of this experience, I heard my voice ask, "Do you think this is literal or symbolic?" And Istvan answered, "Oh, I don't think it's literal, but I don't know why I have to keep on having the same damned experience." I asked, "Do you think that you need to be more accepting of death?" And he answered, "That could be, but I am not going to accept it. I will not give up the power over my own life. Yet, the strange thing was that when I said that to the Great Mother, I had the feeling of agreement from her, as though she was saying, 'Of course, who else would or could have that power? We are all working together and each of us makes choices in cooperation with everyone else working on the earth project.' I knew this was true, but I sure as hell did not accept that my part in the project was dying."

Then Istvan said to me as if it were an afterthought, "Pisti and I merged into one. You know, he has certain qualities that I don't have, and I have certain qualities that he does not have. We are going to have to combine our energies and talents into one in order to do the work that lies ahead." I was surprised that I had not questioned what he meant by this.

That evening Istvan, Jenny, and I went out to eat. Istvan bought a dozen roses for Jenny. He said that in his experience that afternoon Pisti had asked him to take the roses to Jenny as a gift from Pisti. All the roses were to be white except one, which was to be red. The white roses were a symbol of life in the material dimension while the red rose was a symbol for Pisti's life in the spirit dimension. Istvan said that Pisti wanted to help us expand our thinking about death and hoped this symbol would help. "Death," Pisti said, "is as alive as life."

Istvan told Jenny about his struggle with death that afternoon. We all seemed to think it was symbolic. As we ended the discussion though, Jenny and I told Istvan he'd better not die, and Istvan vowed he would not leave us.

Three months later, on February 19, 1994, one day before Istvan left for Hungary where he was killed on March 2, 1994, Istvan had the following experience:

> *As I was lying in bed, I had the feeling that I was surrounded by spirits. The energy was loving, and I felt like they wanted to help me to have confidence. The whole experience was sort of like a confidence builder. They explained to me once again that I needed to relax. I didn't need to try to control anything. Just relax. If I had a question about anything, I just needed to focus on it, and the answer would come quite naturally. I needed to trust the process. Everything was like a review, a reminder.*
>
> *Then I saw the image of earth worms. The spirits said, "Well, these are the earth worms that are transforming your body into new ground." They explained that the new ground would be a*

great Receptor. This made me uncomfortable, and I started turning and twisting. The uneasiness finally went away, but I had the feeling that this *is a process that is already under way – a transformation that is coming and that cannot be stopped.*

They just kept sending confidence to me. I felt them say, "Everything will work out the way it has to be. Don't try to force things. Everything will be just as it has been intended, as we and you have chosen. Whatever happens will be for the benefit of everybody involved. Everything is on schedule."

We had so convinced ourselves that all of the death motifs were symbolic that I was able to say to Istvan, "That is actually beautiful, Istvan. Your transformation has been so radical that your entire body is now a Receptor for new life." And this *was* true. Both of us had experienced, and were continuing to experience, significant transformations. However, since we were focused on our move to the woods, our new life, and whether or not we would have enough money, Istvan's experience helped us to have the confidence that everything would work out. And in fact, Istvan now seemed to have such confidence in life that it didn't seem as though either of us thought about death.

That evening we went out to dinner with friends. While we were eating, it began to rain. After dinner, we said good-bye to our friends and walked in the rain back to our car. When we returned home, Tibi had just arrived from his weekend stay with Paul and Adel. Istvan began packing for his flight early the next day. Then Jenny came by for a few minutes with Dustin, a friend of Jenny's since high school. Dustin and Pisti had also been friends, and during these two years since Pisti's death, Dustin had been a great help to Jenny. Once I had suggested to Jenny that I thought Dustin loved her even beyond the friendship that they shared. But Jenny quickly responded, "Oh, no. I don't think so, and I don't want it that way. I need him as my friend."

Now we all gathered in the living room to look at a photo album Jenny had made for Pisti's grandmother in Hungary. It was filled with pictures of Pisti during the last weeks of his life.

We laughed and talked for quite awhile. It always felt good to have young people together again in our house. When Jenny and Dustin left, Tibi went to his room and Istvan returned to his packing. Suddenly, I was struck with a pervasive sadness. I could not figure out what had hit me. I thought perhaps it was Pisti's absence from a situation in which he would have been so fully present.

I went into the room where Istvan was packing. I asked him if he needed any help. He thought not, but he wanted to show me a tee shirt with a dolphin on the front that he had bought for Anita, a young friend in Hungary. That reminded me of the tapes in English I had made for her that afternoon. I went into my study to get them so he could take them with the shirt. When I returned, I saw that Istvan was well organized, so I just sat down on the floor and talked with him while he packed.

We talked about Anita, who had experienced the death of a close friend in a car accident a few months before Pisti's accident. After his death, she too had powerful experiences about the critical condition of the earth. She was convinced that only a transformation of our consciousness can save the planet. Istvan and I had planned to go to Hungary the coming summer, and I was to meet Anita then. As it turned out, she and I would meet in less than three weeks.

As I sat on the floor of Istvan's office and we continued to talk, my sorrow remained. Istvan usually did not sleep on the night before a flight. He wanted to be able to sleep on the plane so he would arrive in Germany ready to drive to Hungary. However, since I had to work the next day, I decided to go to bed. When I stood up, my unexplained sorrow became too great to contain. I started to cry. I told Istvan that I really did not know why I was crying. We just held each other while we stood in the hallway, but I couldn't stop crying. Finally, Istvan said, "Kicsikém, remember that you are connected now. The bridge is there. Whatever comes, trust it. We *know* what we have experienced is true. It doesn't matter *what* anybody else thinks."

That night Istvan came to bed. My sorrow had now turned into panic. We held each other all night, and eventually I fell asleep. Istvan woke me and Tibi at four the next morning. We both wanted to see him off. The sorrow and panic were gone. In fact, I didn't even think of that evening again until I received the news of Istvan's death.

Later, when I thought about what he had said to me that night in the hallway, I understood that he had spoken out of the depths of the Self who knew he would not return. And Istvan knew well that I would need to be grounded, to trust the transformations, and to live by the wisdom of the visions. *It simply could not matter what anyone else thought or said.* Such visions brought with them a great responsibility.

A few days after I arrived in Hungary, Anita and I met. She and Istvan had eaten dinner together the night of the accident. "He didn't seem quite himself," she said. "He told me he once had a vision that he would one day meet someone who looked exactly like Pisti." Then Istvan had said to her, "I feel as though I'm going to meet that person very soon." Anita felt an unusual intensity in Istvan when he spoke about this. "Sometimes Istvan referred to the person as 'someone who looked like Pisti' and at other times he just called the person 'Pisti.'" We both wondered if, later that night, it actually had been a vision of Pisti that caused Istvan to go off the road.

When I returned home to California, I looked in our records for that vision. It was in May of 1992, almost two years earlier. As I listened to the tape, I heard Istvan's voice say, "A very weird thing happened. Pisti said that I will meet him or someone like him. I will be so startled by such a look-alike that I almost pass out." It seemed possible to me that such a vision might have caused Istvan's accident. It certainly had not made much sense that a driver like Istvan would simply go off the road.

Then one Sunday afternoon about two months after his death, I lay down on the bed in the meditation room. I was filled with questions about the accident. Suddenly, I began to feel the presence of a strong energy in the northwest section of the room. I knew it was Istvan. Then, as if in answer to my questions, I felt him say, "No, I did not have on the safety belt. Yes, I was speeding." And then, more slowly, "Kicsi, it was my night to die. Everything is exactly as it has to be."

Then I "saw" the car flying in the air. Istvan's body was thrown forward through the window and out of the car, but, at the same time, I saw his "soul body" fly through the back side window in the opposite direction. As I watched his soul fly out, I saw Pisti's spirit essence waiting for him. Pisti was more bright light than form, but I felt his arms embrace Istvan as the two very quickly merged and became one. I felt that Istvan was immediately conscious of what had happened with Pisti. But when he now spoke to me, he did not refer to this event. He only said, "That's right, Kicsi, the soul was out of the body before the body hit the ground." While there was nothing in this vision to indicate that Istvan had "seen" Pisti *before* the accident, it did seem that Pisti was present *during* the accident.

I did not think much more about the cause of the accident until one Sunday evening a few weeks later. Istvan's brother Paul had just brought Tibi back to my home from their usual weekend visit. Tibi went into his room while Paul and I went into the kitchen to make some coffee. While Istvan and Paul were very different from each other, there had been a bond between them. I knew that Paul had suffered when Pisti and Istvan died. Yet neither Istvan nor I had ever discussed our unusual experiences with Paul. We both knew how difficult it could be to communicate experience that has been excluded from the rational worldview—a worldview that was not only Paul's heritage but his firmly held conviction. Or so it seemed.

That evening Paul surprised me by saying, "Betty, there's something I'd like to talk to you about." I stopped making coffee. "You know," he continued, "I never dreamed about Pisti after his death. I tried, but I never did. Then last week I dreamed about Pisti *and* Istvan." Paul then told me his dream:

> *I am at the scene of the accident in Szentes. Istvan is sitting on top of the car, which is upside down. A tall young man*

> *wearing sunglasses and dressed in black is standing beside him. I immediately ask Istvan, "How in the hell did you have such a stupid accident?" He smiles and says as he turns to the young man beside him, "He was crowding me!" Then I realize that the young man is Pisti, who now is also smiling. I watch as the two of them walk away together.*

I was astonished to say the least. Astonished that Paul had valued and wanted a dream experience and that his dream had provided another piece of the puzzle about Istvan's accident. I said, "Paul, come sit down. There are some things I'd like to tell you as well." I then told him what Istvan had said to Anita at dinner the night he died and my rather recent meditation experience of the accident. These three pieces of the puzzle about Istvan's accident had come from three different people, and the picture that emerged looked very much as though, on that fatal night, Istvan might indeed have had a vision of someone who looked like Pisti, or was it Pisti? Was the look-alike so real that Istvan almost passed out? Did the vision appear on the highway and actually "crowd" him off the road? However it happened, I knew there had to be quite a powerful conspiracy to get Istvan out of the body "on schedule."

It was true that Pisti and Istvan experienced very quick deaths, but the dreams and visions revealed that the whole process of releasing themselves from matter had been much slower. During the last two years of their lives, both were experiencing an intensification of the life force within them. Yet, at the same time, the deep Mind in all three of us was dreaming of and preparing for their deaths.

The radical transformation that was taking place within Pisti and Istvan opened them to a compassion that was so deeply personal that it connected them to the life of the planet. Istvan's and my experiences with Pisti after his death were focused not only on our own healing but on that of the earth as well. I now felt that part of Istvan's role in the earth project actually was to die in this dimension in order that he and Pisti could, as Istvan had earlier put it, "combine our energies and talents into one in order to do the work that lies ahead." Given all the experiences the three of us had about the earth, I was not able to deny this possibility. And the power of the Milky Way vision was still very much alive in me: the earth had called for its own healing and the response was multidimensional.

Pisti's metaphor of surfing the oceans of life was appropriate for both Pisti and Istvan. They had not always surfed. There had been times when they unconsciously floated, other times when they lost their balance and almost drowned, or crashed but somehow reemerged afloat, and there had been times when they had foolishly dared the waves to overturn them. But finally, near the end of their lives, they were learning how to hold the extremes of life in both hands, to balance themselves, and to ride high on the crest of the life force. They wanted to live each moment fully, and neither of them wanted to let that moment go.

Yet they did. Something deep within had taught them both that birth and death are the breathing out and the breathing in of Life itself. On that deep level they both knew that "there is nothing *but* Life." Istvan understood this in spite of his resistance. One evening not long before his death, Istvan and I were talking about the incredible nature of all we were experiencing. Suddenly, Istvan stopped eating and looked across the table at me. It was one of those moments when individual consciousness pauses and deep Mind flows through and astonishes both speaker and listener. As Istvan spoke, both of us felt the numinous power of his words:

Death is as Divine as Life.
Hold them in both hands, Kicsi.
Play with them.
Balance them.
This is the Divine Game.

Chapter Ten

"Then gradually people all over the earth begin to dance the Round Dance to heal the raped heart."

—The Dreaming Mind

As I begin this tenth—and last—chapter, it is also the tenth year since Istvan and I received that "unexpected call" that brought "the jarring end" of what we had considered normal life. Anubis, God of the Void, the All, had appeared on the horizon and beckoned us to follow him into the Mystery of Death. This "plunge into eternity" had curved the straight line of our mythological Imagination into the wholeness of the circle. We had experienced the Miracle of Death.

Even before the dream (p. 50-51) about people all over the earth dancing the Round Dance to heal the raped heart, there had been other dreams and visions of the healing circle. In 1990, after my first trip to Peru but before the deaths of Mother, Pisti, and Istvan, I had a profoundly painful experience about the earth. Two friends and I had set aside a day of meditation and ritual for our children and the earth. There was no way we could have anticipated the events of that day.

After about an hour of meditation I felt my identity begin to shift slightly away from myself and toward the earth. At the time, this process seemed quite natural, but as the shift was taking place, I began to feel more and more nauseated. One of my friends realized that I was sick and brought me a glass of water. When I tried to drink it, I had to get up to spit it out because it tasted polluted. It was then that I realized that something unusual was taking place, something I had to experience inside my own body. I sat down again and tried to give myself over to the experience.

For quite awhile I experienced a state of tension between the need to regurgitate the pollution inside my body and the desperate need to hold myself in balance. When my identity began to shift back to its normal position, I was profoundly grateful but exhausted. I prayed that I would never forget what I had experienced as an extraordinary act of love on the part of the earth to endure this acute struggle of holding all her systems in balance while being filled with pollutants, both material and mental. However, I knew that the balance had been lost and that a worldwide catastrophe was in process. I knew that life on our planet was in crisis.

I felt such sadness for the earth—a sadness that became a hunger so deep and pervasive that I could not say whether it was physical or spiritual. I felt hopeless. Then this same hunger throughout the planet coagulated into the image of an emaciated mother holding her dying child. The whole world seemed empty. Nothing could ever matter again. *Nothing*. Then I felt a voice say, "This is the Pietà of the earth."

How had we come to this? *How* could we have come to *this*? I knew that the earth did not *have* to be this way. I felt a voice answer me, "You forgot." These words seemed to echo through the long tunnel of my unconsciousness and reverberate back to me: "You forgot. You forgot."

I knew by now what I had forgotten—what we all had forgotten. But I had not realized how much it mattered. The great shift in my perspective of myself had been in the vision of 1989 (p. 72-73) when I *remembered* who I am, who we all are, and even then I still responded, "But I can't create a world!" I thought now about the reply to that response: "You just did create a world in which you cannot create! We can do nothing but create." In the ecstasy that had followed that awareness, I had shouted my creation to the universe: I would create better games, games where all our children would be nurtured and healed, where they could remember that they are creators and where they could know the ecstasy, love, and joy that we all are so capable of experiencing.

But in our amnesia, we had "forgotten" ourselves into a "terrible dream" where neither mother nor child is nurtured. How had we fallen into this amnesia? How had we lost our self-esteem? How had we lost the understanding that our ego was to be the mirror of our inner uniqueness flowing out of universal Mind? How had we turned this ego "wrong-side out" so that it had to go snatching and grabbing from the outer world anything that would make us feel good about ourselves? And how had we been able to forget the creative power in every thought and feeling and longing?

I knew that there were people all over the planet who wanted to create themselves out of this nightmare, but it was so easy to feel defeated. What I did not know then, but was just about to experience, was the unlimited power of this collective longing.

As I remained seated on the floor with my eyes closed, I "saw" in "the inner space and time of consciousness" a very large circular object appear out of the southern sky and move through the closed sliding glass doors of the room where I was sitting. This disk of radiant conscious light hovered directly above my head. Its powerful energy gently pulled my body into an upright position. Suddenly, a spiral of light flowed very quickly out of the bottom center of the disk and simultaneously shaped itself into the form of a woman who spiraled into my body through the center of my head. The movement was so quick that I could catch only a glimpse of her from her head to her breast. She wore a fitted white satin dress and a white satin four-cornered hat. I was aware that the four corners of her hat and the circle of the disk formed a beautiful mandala, an ancient symbol of wholeness.

Then she began to sing through me. I do not sing well, but the voice seemed to me to be quite beautiful. I was aware that she had taken form for two reasons: by entering my Imagination, she could create a reality in the world of material space and time, and she could transform the currency of the multidimensional consciousness within the disk to a frequency that I could carry. By doing this, she made it possible for me to experience this light and consciousness and love as a unified field of energy. The friends in the room with me did not see the disk or the woman, but they felt the presence of her energy. When she sang, she addressed all three of us:

You have called us
And we are here
To be with you all three.

Can you feel us?
You have called us
And we are here.

We are the Light.
We are the Light
Circling around your planet.

Can you feel us?
Your planet has called us
And we are here.

Her presence filled me with knowledge far beyond her words: I *knew* that this energy field had been collecting around our planet for a very long time and that every person who had ever longed for love and a more meaningful life had drawn this energy around the earth. I also knew that this longing had now reached the critical mass necessary to pull this hovering energy field directly to the earth itself.

I heard the Voice announce that "they" were ready to connect to our planet. I felt energy flow through me and into the earth. I then realized that the three of us were seated in a circle with our arms around each other. Each of us had intuitively felt that we needed to do this at this moment. Then the Voice addressed the three of us again:

You have drawn to yourselves this day
All those on your planet
Who are creating worlds
Of Love and Peace.

Then the female form spiraled back up and into the disk of light, which moved out through the glass doors and toward the mountains to the North. Each of us was left with the feeling that, in some unexplainable way, it had been our destiny to participate in this sacred earth ritual with all the other people on our planet who had longed for worlds of Love and Peace. I still had a long journey ahead of me, but this vision was a jewel that reminded me again and again of the power of every single person's love, grief, and longing to create a better world for ourselves and our children.

I returned home late that afternoon. Istvan was out of town and Pisti was waiting for me because he needed some extra money for that evening. We talked awhile, but I did not tell him what had happened. When he left, I showered and lay down on the bed. I felt as though I was in a state of shock. As time passed, my rational mind began to assert itself and attempt to dismiss the visit of the radiant being as impossible. Yet the reality of the experience had been so powerful that even my programmed rational mind was having trouble dismissing it. Finally, in a state of exhaustion, I fell asleep and had the following dream:

> *I am in Budapest. I am holding a round, flat sieve with small pebbles on it. As I gently and thoughtfully shake it, a disembodied hand abruptly appears and rakes off the pebbles. Then a voice says, "These do not belong in the city."*
>
> *The scene changes. I am in the very heart of the city. An artist has gathered the discarded pebbles and created a work of art by placing these stones in a circle. I, along with many other people in the city, am circling around them. We walk in silence because we are in a deep state of observation and contemplation. The mind, body, and heart are focused on this work of art. The atmosphere is charged with creative energy. Then, suddenly, I realize that these pebbles are not pebbles at all: they are the very large standing stones of antiquity. I feel the sacredness of their power.*

This dream came as a gift to my confused and shocked mind. Certainly, it was an accurate reflection of my rational mind before the coming decade of initiation and transformation—the disembodied hand, the trained dismissal of excluded realities. Yet it was also a confirmation of the artist in me who would not dismiss experience that did not fit or "belong" in the Western paradigm of reality—the city as opposed to nature. And the dream gave me permission to honor my experience, not by trying to prove it but by artistically shaping it so that the whole mind could be activated.

At first, I wondered why the city was Budapest. Then I remembered that Budapest is actually Buda and Pest divided by a river. When the artist created her work in the "heart" of this city, she was integrating the two parts at their vital center. She had gathered together what the rational mind had excluded and arranged the pieces in such a way—a circle—that the whole mind—the whole city—was captivated and inspired. The rational mind had been able to see only useless pebbles while the whole mind experienced the magnificence of the sacred standing stones. *The artist understood that the whole mind was required for reality to reveal its essential nature.*

It was certainly true that my whole mind had been captivated and inspired by all the dreams and visions. Out of this wholeness of mind, I had been able to experience a quality and depth in life that created a context for both joy and sorrow. Yet, unlike Istvan, I had to exercise extreme caution in order to maintain a balanced cooperation between the rational and symbolic functions of my mind. As a teacher of literary art forms, I had been trained in this kind of balance: to experience, observe, and contemplate a work of art and then to allow a respectful dialogue to emerge between the art form and the analytic mind. It was truly ironic that in the past I had been able to do this for the work of every other artist except the living artist within myself.

Therefore, I vowed that I would not allow my rational mind to devalue, dismiss, or reject any symbolic dream or visionary experience. Such an experience was a work of art that invited my whole mind to circle around it in observation and contemplation. Any lesser response would not only be a rejection of my inner artist but a cowardly denial of my own intelligence. To the degree that I was successful in allowing a respectful communication between these two mental functions, the rational mind excelled in reasonableness and the symbolic mind startled me with its creativity.

Vico was correct in his assessment of the appropriate relationship between the symbol and the captivated rational mind when he said that the symbol cannot be reduced to an idea any more than the idea can be reduced to a symbol. The symbol or myth is not undeveloped: it exists as a fully developed form of language in and of itself, as does the idea or conceptual language. For the whole mind to be captivated and engaged, we must allow these two languages to meet on equal ground where neither language can control, dominate, or transform its opposite into itself. Such a ground makes it possible to create a relationship of "tension and dialectic" between the symbol and the idea.[1]

My experiences left me certain that the earth was dreaming a myth of just such creative relationships where all opposing principles could meet on equal ground. Such a myth is born out of our deepest aspirations to create experiences of love and respect, not only with each other but with the earth and the universe. Within such a myth all life is nourished, for it is consistent with "the essential structure of the universe." And since this structure is the ground of all creation, this myth will be multidimensional and far larger than any one culture's view of reality.

I knew that the dreams and visions that Istvan and I had experienced were integral, interrelated, living pieces of this vast, multidimensional myth that is still in the process of dreaming itself into material reality throughout the planet. I felt certain that this myth reflects symbolically the "wave of organization" that is moving through human consciousness and forming what Thompson calls a "new planetary culture."

Perhaps the most radical aspect of this new mentality that we had glimpsed is that it allows us to experience ourselves as the creative energy within this "wave of organization," to know ourselves as immanental Mind. The earth has been trying to dream this "wave of organization" into consciousness for centuries. All of the world's great religions and all of the earth's indigenous spiritual traditions reflect to a greater or lesser degree this great dream of the earth.

One of the most persistent and worldwide symbols for this dream is the Round Dance. This spiraling dance is the most sacred of all rituals because it curves the straight line of our mythological Imagination into the wholeness of the circle. Here, the dead ends of the straight line are fused and consciousness takes a qualitative leap into multidimensional possibilities.

As we dance this spiral dance to the center of our deepest selves, we confront the divine, the Cosmic Mind, the All—*not as Other, but as Self.* It is here, in total and unconditional love, that we remember who we are. All apparent oppositions reveal to us that they "are not two different states, but they are different aspects of the same state." It is here that we remember that there is nothing but life, and that we are "the nucleus of the nucleus" of that life.

According to the Gnostic gospel, *Acts of St. John,* Jesus danced the Round Dance. Christ stood in the middle, and his apostles danced around him in a circle. They chanted what were thought to be "magical formulas" that, with the circular dance, effected a deep meditative state and the experience of oneness with the Divine. One of the more "recurrent though much varied" formulas that was chanted as they danced was "Thou art I and I am thou."[2]

Jesus thus left his disciples a ritual to be used to achieve and maintain consciousness of their own divinity. Through this practice we would not forget who we are, and the earth dream could be kept alive. In another Gnostic text, "Gospel of Thomas," Jesus said,

> *I am not your master. Because you have drunk, you have become intoxicated from the bubbling spring which I have measured out. . . . He who will drink from My mouth will become like Me. I myself shall become he, and the things that are hidden will be revealed to him.*[3]

But for so long we have excluded from our reality "the things that are hidden." It seemed to me now, however, that "the things that are hidden" were determined to reveal themselves. Of course, there always had been those who, like Jesus, had held in compassionate consciousness that which had been hidden to most of the world. They had been like points of light on the planet. Now, however, the longing all over the planet had become so great that it had drawn to itself an energy field of light, consciousness, and love.

If it is true that a critical mass on our planet has opened itself to this powerful light energy, then it is also true that we have opened ourselves to the suffering and darkness of our planet. Consciousness and love emit a revealing light. When the depth of that suffering and the intensity of the violence within that suffering become apparent to us, we will hear the Voice in the desert scream out across the dunes that "It can never be healed!"

But now the Voice of Darkness and the Voice of Light exist together on equal ground within the alembic of our souls. This is potentially the most creative relationship of our lives, for this is a relationship of all that has been suffered and feared but that now is grounded in conscious, loving light. In this relationship we are able to confront our greatest fears: the fear that life and death are without meaning—and the fear of our own personal darkness. And this, of course, is why we called Anubis, the Master of both Darkness and Light.

Anubis came to announce the death of our worldview. He came to announce *our* death. In fact, it was Anubis *who had called us.* He had called us into the circle of Life, for he is that circle. Yet he beckons us to enter this circle at the gate of death and dissolution, to follow him into the Void of no-thingness and nonbeing. As we enter that gate, he will offer us his "knowledge beyond books."

We accept this knowledge and, as the darkness of Anubis penetrates us, we begin to feel the waves of dissolution flowing through us. Old patterns, ideas, feelings, beliefs—our *realities*—are softened, dissolved, and then, gradually, released. We welcome this dissolution, for our identity is no longer within these structures. Something greater in us is being loved by the universe, and it is in the light of this love that we are now able to see the contamination the old structures have caused. So we set out on our journey, embraced always by this light, to the North Pole to visit the great earth cauldrons of unclaimed pollution. We take what belongs to us, and we begin the work that is poisonous to most, but for a jackal is life-giving.

The Great Anubis has opened the "Way" and we have entered the space between worlds. Slowly, we begin to feel the vastness of this space, and its emptiness flows through us. We wait, for we know that it will be out of this "fecund emptiness" that we will give birth to "our true nature." This is the *Miracle* that recreates the world.

On March 16, 1992, a few months after Pisti's death, Istvan also had an experience of the presence and the power of this field of light that embraces and supports our work to find "our true nature."

One evening Istvan felt Pisti's presence, and he sensed that Pisti wanted to show him something. As soon as he had registered that thought, he and Pisti were looking at the earth from a distance in space that allowed Istvan to see a radiant light hovering just above the earth's surface all around the globe. Pisti explained that this light was attracted to the planet by everyone on the planet who had ever loved. They moved closer to the earth, and Istvan began to feel the intensity of his own love and grief for Pisti. "Dad," Pisti said, "the power of this love can do anything. It is infinite."

Istvan then realized that just beneath the light there was what appeared to be an impenetrable layer of pollution that encrusted the earth like cement. Istvan had begun to feel the force of this negation when he heard Pisti say, "Only love can pierce the pollution of forgetfulness, separation, and despair that covers the earth." Then Pisti said, "Dad, can you see those points of light all around the globe?" Istvan looked closer and was surprised that within the field of light he now could see individual points of concentrated light. "Those points," Pisti said, "are formed by the soul energy of the Jackal Healers."

I asked Istvan what he thought Pisti meant, and Istvan said that the Jackal Healers were souls who had achieved the ability to hold and to transmit powerful forms of energy, "sort of like high-voltage power stations. I realized," Istvan said, "that the most powerful energy in the universe is love, and that those souls were able to receive, hold, and transmit the light of love that I saw hovering just above the earth." Then Istvan added, "Pisti said that everyone who loves is dreaming a dream to pierce that pollution and carry this light to the center of the earth."

Istvan and I knew that Pisti was trying to communicate something to us that could not be stated in conceptual language, so we tried to stay with the metaphor and allow it to unfold within us during the weeks and months that followed. I kept thinking about those people all over the planet who were healing the earth through their love, but who probably were unaware of their power and creativity.

I also thought about my own past visions of the light around the planet, and then of the light connecting to the planet. And now, not in a vision of mine but in Istvan's vision, the light was penetrating the planet. Only later, when I was transcribing the visions, would I realize that Istvan's powerful "film" vision (p. 96-97) also related similar information: love and the longing for love had created enough energy "to hold the beam of light that is coming." It seemed that the earth truly was dreaming a dream of "infinite possibilities."

Istvan's experience of the Jackal Healers transmitting light reminded me of an earlier but sad experience of my own when I was still paralyzed with doubt. I was able to "see" how my body could not hold or transmit the light that was flowing through the universe: as the light touched me, it was immediately absorbed into the darkness of my doubt. This was a painful experience, but it helped me to move into a space of conscious responsibility where I could work on dissolving the patterns, ideas, feelings, beliefs, and *realities* that prevented me from participating in a multidimensional worldview.

This experience also helped me to understand Pisti's statement that the points of concentrated light were Jackal Healers: souls who could hold and transmit light *because* they had transformed their own darkness and made room in themselves for the light. They were "Openers of the Way" for the light to flow from point to point all over the globe.

Istvan and I were convinced that these visions of light were a reflection of the work taking place on the deep levels of consciousness. The earth now had the grounding of this unified field of love so that we would be able to "Work on What Has Been Spoiled." This was a work, as Wilhelm emphasized in his commentary on this hexagram, that could be accomplished only if love prevailed and extended over both the beginning and the end.

Even before his death, Pisti felt that the earth was working toward a new level of development. One afternoon he came into my study and asked if I had time for a break. I said I did, so he sat down. Had Pisti and I not had a tradition of honoring and discussing dreams and symbolic experiences, I would never have known about his dreams of death or what he was about to tell me now. Pisti explained that the evening before he had had an out-of-body experience. He said he had been sitting on the side of his bed working on a drawing when he began to hear a loud buzzing sound as if something were moving in a circle. "Then," he said, "I somehow knew I was going to go out of my body. I lay down on the bed, and as soon as I looked at the wall, it was gone. I shot out of my body and into the stars. The very moment that I had the thought, 'My God! I'm out of my body,' I was back in my room, but not in my body. I was standing in the middle of the room looking at my body lying on the bed. I saw a large child being born out of my heart. I didn't know what to make of that, but while I was wondering about it, I shot back out into the night."

As he moved through space, he observed black holes, "star systems," and what he called the movement of "space groups" of parallel worlds. When he realized I was having some difficulty understanding all that he had experienced, he made drawings of each one. Then he said, "I was in a parallel world that was like this world." He started laughing and said, "In fact, my bathroom still had the same leaky toilet that Dad hasn't fixed yet. Everything was the same except it seemed deeper and more lush. But the feeling was completely different: I knew there were no limits to creativity. *It was a world in balance.*" Then after awhile, he added, "You know, Mom, I think that we are working here in this world to create that world there."

I had not previously thought about a connection between this experience of Pisti's and Istvan's vision in which Pisti asked him to find my copy of *The I Ching* and read the hexagram about working on that which has spoiled or decayed. Pisti had asked Istvan to read the hexagram carefully because it delineated our work and the work of the earth. I read again my notes from that day, "You know, Mom, I think that we are working here in this world to create that world there." It was one thing to think about the transformative power of distilling the darkness into light, but it was quite another to think that Pisti actually had visited the world that this work could bring into being. I went back to *The I Ching* to read Wilhelm's commentary once again with this new perspective.

Wilhelm states that the ruler of the hexagram is the fifth line moving from bottom to top, "for although all of the lines are occupied in compensating for what has been spoiled, it is only at the fifth line that the work is completed. Hence all of the other lines have warnings appended to them, and only of the fifth is it said: 'One meets with praise.'" Thus the work is completed, and the world is set in order.[4]

But what about the sixth line? This line, we are told, is "strong" and at "the highest point" of the hexagram. "Therefore it does not serve the king in the fifth place but sets its goals higher. It does not work for one era, but for the world and for all time."[5] Thus it would appear that by the fifth line, we have learned how to distill the polluted darkness into light and to achieve the order and balance necessary for creative relatedness. Now our energies can rise to the sixth line where we are capable of setting our goals even higher.

When Istvan first told me that ML identified the lines in the hexagram from the top to the bottom, I did not think much about it other than to say that the hexagram is traditionally read from the bottom to the top. Now I could see the symbolic significance in the flowing of ML from the top to the bottom since our own work begins from the bottom of the hexagram and rises to the top. We had called this light to ourselves and through our work we would rise to meet it. At the sixth level, we too would be Masters of Light who work "for the world and for all time." "But," as Istvan said, "there is a lot of work to be done."

And as we enter into this work, we will be entering into that "desperately and urgently required project for our time"—the exploration of "the inner space and time of consciousness." This work is rooted in the life of the visionary and the mystic, for it is life within Mind that is primary. It is the vision that creates and recreates the world. When we look at the outer world and grieve, we do not believe that this outer reality is separated from our inner reality: we know we are looking at the limitations of our visions. We do not say that we cannot change this world. Rather, we say we must have the courage to live within the creative power of our visions.

Fortunately, as mentioned earlier, science is now able to strengthen this courage. Physicist Fred Alan Wolf speaks of a "physics of the spirit" that is emerging in our culture. "Quantum physics," says Wolf, "shows us that matter is how spirit appears in the physical universe."

> *The tracks left by subatomic particles in our sophisticated detecting devices reveal the presence of a non-physical reality temporarily manifesting as physical substance. When we investigate matter at its deepest level, we find it dissolving into a non-substantial reality that religion calls spirit. In fact, quantum physics teaches us that there's no fundamental difference between matter and spirit.*[6]

On May 23, 1992, Istvan's first birthday after Pisti's death, I had a beautiful vision in which Jenny, Istvan, Pisti, and I celebrated the inseparable Oneness of spirit and matter:

I am standing in the South and looking straight ahead toward the North. I am waiting for Pisti to arrive. Suddenly, I feel his presence, but I do not see him. Then I have a feeling that something incredible is about to happen, and in that moment, Pisti becomes visible.

He is dressed in Native American clothes made from soft white doeskin. I realize that I too am dressed in the same white doeskin. Then I see that Jenny is standing in the East and Istvan in the West. They are both wearing soft brown doeskin clothing. The four of us symbolize the four corners that form the sacred circle. Behind Pisti are mountains, and I notice that the ground in the North is of a slightly higher elevation than the other three positions.

Istvan, Jenny, and I are looking toward Pisti. We know that the ritual we are about to perform is sacred. Slowly, Pisti lifts the long and magnificent Native American pipe, and he calls forth the energies of the four corners of the earth. The energies of the South, the West, then the North and the East arrive. It is a powerful moment. The silence is penetrating. The moment is eternal.

Then Pisti slowly walks from the North to the East. He stands before Jenny. Each of us feels the power of their love. Pisti smokes the pipe and then presents it to Jenny. As she too smokes the sacred pipe, Pisti chants in a voice that resonates in every cell, "Spirit and Matter are One." Then he walks to the South, and we all experience the love that Pisti and I have for each other. He repeats the pipe ritual and chant. Then he walks to the West and stands before Istvan. All of us experience the love Istvan and Pisti have for each other. The pipe ritual is repeated again, and the chant resonates in the air, "Spirit and Matter are One." Then Pisti returns to the North, and the energy of the sacred circle flows through us just as the spirit smoke of the sacred pipe and the tones of the chant flow through us.

Here, within this sacred circle, I know that Sira and Hermes Trismegistus are part of "the essential structure of the universe." Sira is one of the infinite number of names for the Divine Play of Love. She, Love, is the "Force behind the Force of Pure Creativity"; she is the "Force of Pure Creativity" and she is "Pure Creativity." We are all Sira.

And we are all her beloved Hermes Trismegistus. His name is one of the infinite number of names for the twin energy of all Polarities as they dance through the Great Loom on which Reality is strung. He is the dance between the two, and he maintains the balance of that dance. It is this "exquisite balance" that opens the way to the Power of Three – Thrice-Greatest Hermes – the eternal unity of all things in the universe.

During that summer of 1992 Jenny, Istvan, and I decided to go to Mount Shasta to take some of Pisti's ashes and to celebrate the sacred ritual he had taught us. Since we had never been to this area before, we did not know exactly where we would go, but we planned simply to follow our intuition. We stopped in a small shop before beginning our ascent. As we were leaving the shop, the woman who owned the shop said, "Don't miss Panther Meadows. That's a very powerful place." Panther Meadows! We had no idea there was such a place. We now felt as though Pisti's black panther had jumped off his arm and was leading us up the mountain.

As soon as we arrived in Panther Meadows, we began to look for just the right place for our ceremony. I found a place, but Jenny and Istvan thought we could do better, so we continued to look. Suddenly, Jenny came running toward us to tell us she had found the perfect spot. When Istvan and I saw it, we agreed. We all began to make the necessary preparations. Then we took our positions to form the sacred circle.

Istvan walked from his position in the West to the North and performed the ceremony with the pipe as Pisti had done in my vision. After the ceremony, I was astonished to realize that mountains could be seen in the North and that the land in that direction was of a slightly higher elevation even within the circle. This was exactly how the layout had been in the vision. I had not mentioned this to anyone because it had not seemed particularly significant—even though I had wondered at the time why that kind of detail would be in the vision. Now I knew. I told Jenny and Istvan. Istvan laughed and said, "Well, Jenny, your intuition is right on."

Much later, after Istvan's death and my return from Hungary, Jenny and I met to talk about Istvan and the night he died. She told me that she had come home late that night. When she entered her bedroom, she had the definite feeling that she was not alone. She got ready for bed, turned off the light, and lay down. The sense of presence became stronger. Then she felt Pisti at her side, but she also felt the energy of someone else up near the ceiling. As she lay there, the presence above her increased in intensity until it became so powerful that it could not be ignored, yet she did not know what to do.

> *I knew this energy wasn't going to hurt me, but it was so strong and different from anything I had ever experienced that I became anxious and found myself trying to ignore it. I turned over on my side to try to go to sleep, but the energy next to me, which was definitely Pisti, touched my arm. I quickly turned over on my back again and then Pisti began to gently stroke my face. I knew that he was trying to calm me down.*
>
> *I opened my eyes, but the ceiling was not there. It was as though that section of the ceiling did not exist in the material world. There was just space, but it felt like a doorway. I was able to see the universe through that opening. In that moment I knew that there were no limits to what we can create, but the source of that knowledge was so powerful that I could not continue to look at it. I closed my eyes.*
>
> *Then the phone rang. It was morning, and Jill was calling to tell me that Istvan was dead.*

Jenny did not offer any further comment about this event other than to repeat that the experience had been too powerful for her to look at for more than a moment. We sat for awhile in silence. Then Jenny said, "Betty, I do have something else to tell you. Something that will make you happy." Then she told me that she and Dustin realized that they loved each other. "Finally," I thought to myself, but to Jenny I said, "Nothing could make me happier than to receive this news."

Dustin shared Jenny's worldview, not because it was Jenny's, but because life had brought him his own unusual experiences. Dustin once said to me about these experiences—some painful, others extraordinary—that they helped him see "that everything is connected with everything else. Nothing is left out. Even what I considered negative in my life, I can now see, taught me what really matters. It helps me create the kind of life that is fulfilling. In many of these experiences I had feelings and thoughts that were not at all familiar to me, and they were meaningful. I also learned that creativity is unlimited."

After Pisti's death, Dustin told me that there had been an agreement among four of the guys in their group that whoever died first would get in touch with the others. Within two years of Pisti's death, all of them had contact with Pisti, either through a dream, a visionary experience, or a synchronistic event. During the last years of Pisti's life, I was aware of how these guys met at a local restaurant, drank coffee, and talked for hours, or they went up to the mountains, sat around a fire, and talked all night. Recently, I related to Dustin that now that I was not so focused on the day-to-day concerns of a parent, I was able to realize that their group was quite unusual. Dustin laughed and said, "Yes, that's what brought us together. While other guys were going to football games, we were talking about dying."

I asked Dustin if he realized just how strange that sounded. He laughed again and said, "That does sound pretty funny, doesn't it." And I asked, "Why? Why death and dying?" And then Dustin said something that should not have surprised me, but it did. "Death is the one big mystery that solves everything else." I said, "Stop, wait, I have to write that down exactly as you've said it. That's the theme of my book."

It seemed amazing to me that these teenagers had focused on the one great mystery that was "The Opener of the Way" to all those *realities* that our culture had denied and excluded. I knew that they had discussed many of the excluded realities, but they certainly had been pushing at the edges of our worldview in their pursuit of the mystery of death. They knew that if consciousness survived death, then consciousness was multidimensional. As Pisti's friend Woody recently said to me, "We were definitely looking for other worlds."

Conrad, another friend, agreed: "We were exploring alternatives to what we were being told about death—and just about everything else. We wanted to know why there was war and so much hatred. We were convinced that there were other realities of consciousness that could change this—and we were looking for those realities. We were looking for something 'spiritually' that could heighten consciousness. The problem was that our inner experiences had no validation in the outer world so we didn't know what to do with them. This is what made it difficult." The life experiences of these young men had created in each of them an urgent need "to explore the inner space and time of consciousness." But they also knew that they had to learn to deal with the outer world—in one way or another.

The young mind knows there is a far greater reality than our culture dares to acknowledge. And the young are willing to take risks, "to plunge into eternity," and to explore anything that is denied. In earlier, traditional cultures, it was precisely at this time in a young person's life that the elders prepared the initiation of the young into the secrets of the tribe and of the universe. Until we, the elders of our contemporary culture, can discover, experience, and prepare ourselves to "open the way" in our culture for the young not only to experience the mysteries of the universe but to be able to weave these mysteries into their daily lives, we will continue to lose far too many of them to mediocrity, addiction, violence, indifference, and fanaticism.

I read again "The Judgment" in the hexagram:

WORK ON WHAT HAS BEEN SPOILED

Has supreme success.
It furthers one to cross the great water.

The visions reveal that the foundation has been laid for our work, and *The I Ching* tells us that this work can have supreme success. But we are also told that the work itself must be done with great "decisiveness" and "energy" in order to overcome the pervasive "indifference" and "rigid inertia" in ourselves and in our culture. And we need to act before the consequences of our inaction "acquire a power so overwhelming" that we will stand impotent before them.

Of course, each of us has a different work, and each of us will go about our work in a different way. It is important to remember that we have already started on our journey when we find ourselves asking, "How am I to do this work?" This question indicates that our deepest aspirations for a better world have already set us on our course. Gradually, we come to realize that these very aspirations are pulling us like a magnet into the transformative energy of "the essential structure of the universe." Here we find our true creativity, and it is each person's creativity that is needed to keep the earth balanced.

As we reconnect, full circle, to the roots of our existence in the Mind of the universe, we too will begin to feel the exquisite balance of Persephone: here we will remember that we too are bonded both to birth and to death—to form and to nonform. Here we too hold them in both hands exquisitely "balanced against one another." Here, at the roots of our existence, we experience the deep unity of birth and death, and we experience the radical creativity of both. We understand that "Death is as Divine as Life" because it *is* Life—because "There is nothing *but* Life."

Endnotes

Introduction

1. See Chapter 3, page 38; Chapter 5, pages 81-82; and page 173.

2. Quoted by Robert Lawlor, Translator's Introduction, *Symbol and the Symbolic: Egypt, Science and the Evolution of Consciousness*, by R.A. Schwaller de Lubicz (Brookline: Autumn Press/Random House, Inc., 1978) 16.

3. A. Robert Caponigri, *Time and Idea: The Theory of History in Giambattista Vico* (London: Routledge and Kegan Paul Ltd., 1953) 164-187.

4. Caponigri 164-187.

5. Walter T. Stace, ed., *The Teachings of the Mystics: Selections from the Great Mystics and Mystical Writings of the World* (New York: Mentor Books/The New American Library of World Literature, Inc., 1960) 14-15, 237.

6. Vince Rause, "The Biology of Belief," *Los Angeles Times Magazine* July 15, 2001: 10-13, 33-35 and Andrew Newberg, Eugene d'Aquili and Vince Rause, *Why God Won't Go Away: Brain Science and the Biology of Belief* (New York: Ballantine Books/Random House, Inc., 2001) 7.

7. Newberg 60, 57, 86-90.

8. Newberg 146-147.

9. Gary E.R. Schwartz and Linda G.S. Russek, *The Living Energy Universe: a fundamental discovery that transforms science and medicine* (Charlottesville: Hampton Roads Publishing Company, Inc., 1999) xx, 5-6, 11-12.

10. See Paul H. Ray and Sherry Ruth Anderson, *The Cultural Creatives: How 50 Million People Are Changing the World* (New York: Harmony Books/Random House, Inc., 2000).

11. Rainer Maria Rilke, *Briefe an einen jungen Dichter* (Leipzig: Insel-Verlag, 1932) 46. This passage from Letter Eight translated by Betty J. Kovács.

Chapter One

1. Margaret Marsh is a friend and former colleague. She wrote these words in a note to Istvan and me after our son's death.

2. C.G. Jung and C. Kerényi, *Essays on a Science of Mythology: The Myths of the Divine Child and the Divine Maiden*, trans. R.F.C. Hull (New York: Harper Torch Books/Harper & Row, Publishers, 1963) 104, 106. For many years my thinking had been influenced by the Hungarian Classical scholar, Carl Kerényi. In his essay, "Kore," in *Essays on a Science of Mythology*, Kerényi speaks of the "budlike capacity" of a mythological image "to unfold and yet to contain a whole compact world in itself."

3. Susanne K. Langer, "On Cassirer's Theory of Language and Myth," *The Philosophy of Ernst Cassirer*, ed. Paul Arthur Schilpp (La Salle: Open Court Publishing Company, 1973) 396-397.

Chapter Two

1. R.D. Laing, *The Politics of Experience* (New York: Pantheon Books, 1967) 126-127.

2. From Pisti's journal and my notes of his narration of the dream, 1983.

3. Laing 127.

Chapter Three

1. Gustaf Strömberg, *The Soul of the Universe* (North Hollywood: Educational Research Institute, 1965) 303-305. Strömberg, a Mount Wilson astronomer, wrote as early as 1948 in an appendix to *The Soul of the Universe*, "I believe that behind the physical world we see with our eyes and study in our microscopes and telescopes, and measure with instruments of various kinds, is another, more fundamental realm which can not be described in physical terms. In this non-physical realm lies the ultimate origin of all things, of energy, matter, organization and life, and even of consciousness itself." He describes fields of organization as nature's intelligent, "highly organized activity" that determines the structure of a living body, its disorganization, and its reorganization. "All living organisms are imbedded in complex electric fields, and these fields disappear at death." Strömberg also states that Dr. H.S. Burr, leader of research on fields of organization at Yale Medical School, concluded that "it is hard to escape the conclusion that these fields are independent of the matter involved and by their innate properties determine the structure and functions of the living organism."

2. Lawlor 13-15. See also John Anthony West, *Serpent in the Sky: The High Wisdom of Ancient Egypt* (Wheaton: The Theosophical Publishing House, 1993) 131.

3. Kerényi, "Kore" 107. Kerényi uses these phrases to describe the mythological image of Persephone.

4. Veronica Ions, *Egyptian Mythology* (New York: Peter Bedrick Books, 1982) 82.

5. Arthur Versluis, *The Egyptian Mysteries* (New York: Arkana/Routledge, 1988) 61.

6. Lawlor 14.

7. Kerényi, "Kore" 154.

Chapter Four

No Endnotes

Chapter Five

1. Haridas Chaudhuri, *California Institute of Integral Studies: Fall 98 Public Programs* (San Francisco: CIIS, 1998) 25.

2. C. Kerényi, *Eleusis: Archetypal Image of Mother and Daughter,* trans. Ralph Manheim (New York: Pantheon Books/Bollingen Foundation, 1967) 10-16.

3. Ervin Laszlo, Stanislav Grof, and Peter Russell, *The Consciousness Revolution: A Translatlantic Dialogue,* ed. Ervin Laszlo (Boston: Element Books, Inc., 1999) 17.

4. Kerényi, *Eleusis* 10, 15.

5. Kerényi, "Kore" 120.

6. Johann Wolfgang von Goethe, *Goethes Werke,* textkritisch durchgesehen und kommentiert von Erich Trunz, Band 1 (München: Verlag C.H. Beck, 1974) 358 ("Heilig öffentlich Geheimnis").

7. Betty Kovács, "Journey of the Mothers," *Earthwalking Sky Dancers: Women's Pilgrimages to Sacred Places,* ed. Leila Castle (Berkeley: Frog, Ltd., 1996) 199-201.

8. Kerényi, "Kore" 107.

9. Brian Swimme, *The Hidden Heart of the Cosmos: Humanity and the New Story* (Maryknoll: Orbis Books, 1996) 91-93.

10. Swimme 84-85.

11. Swimme 85-86.

12. William Irwin Thompson, *Imaginary Landscape: Making Worlds of Myth and Science* (New York: St. Martin's Press, 1989) 108.

13. Thompson 93.

14. Thompson 42. See Thompson 3-42 for a detailed discussion of the fairy tale "Rapunzel" as an example of such a document. See also Hertha von Dechend and Giorgio de Santillana, *Hamlet's Mill: An Essay on Myth and the Frame of Time* (Boston: Gambit, 1969).

15. Thompson 41.

16. See Caitlín Matthews, "The Voices of the Wells: Celtic Oral Themes in Grail Literature," *At the Table of the Grail*, ed. John Matthews (London: Watkins Publishing, 2002) 3-25.

17. Amit Goswami, Richard E. Reed, and Maggie Goswami, *The Self-Aware Universe: how consciousness creates the material world* (New York: Jeremy P. Tarcher/Putnam Book, 1995) xvi, xi.

18. Fred Alan Wolf, "Foreword," *Self-Aware Universe* xiv.

19. Goswami 2.

20. Thompson xviii, xiii. For further perspectives on global consciousness, see "Further Reading" and "Organizations for Global Change."

21. Thompson xx.

22. Thompson xx.

23. Laszlo 26.

24. Swimme 108-109.

25. Thompson 136.

26. Thompson xx-xxi.

27. Swimme 71-72.

28. Swimme 74, 73.

29. See Ralph H. Abraham, *Chaos, Gaia, Eros: A Chaos Pioneer Uncovers the Three Great Streams of History* (San Francisco: Harper San Francisco/Harper Collins Publishers, 1994) in which Abraham discusses three recent innovations in the sciences—the Chaos Revolution, Gaia Hypothesis, and Erodynamics—as the reemergence of three branches of ancient wisdom that have been excluded from the Western conception of reality. See also Riane Eisler's *The Chalice and the Blade: Our History, Our Future* (San Francisco: Harper & Row, Publishers, 1987) in which Eisler shows how recent archaeological discoveries about prehistoric cultures reveal just how much "history" has been excluded from the historical model of reality. In my doctoral dissertation, "The Return of the Goddess Creatrix in German Romanticism: A Challenge to the Masculine Trinity of Western Consciousness," University of California, Irvine, 1987, I trace the cycle of repression and reemergence of "excluded realities" throughout the history of Western consciousness.

30. Laing 144 (Laing paraphrases Mallarmé: "L'enfant abdique son extase.")

31. Thompson 83.

32. Thompson 83.

33. Caponigri 164-187.

34. Thompson 96, 82.

35. Dianne Skafte, *Listening to the Oracle: The Ancient Art of Finding Guidance in the Signs and Symbols All Around Us* (New York: Harper San Francisco/Harper Collins Publishers, 1997) 15.

36. Thompson 80.

37. Thompson 83.

38. "Jeder Man soll eine Bibel schreiben."

39. Thompson 48, 47.

Chapter Six

1. Rob Whitesides-Woo, *Miracles.*

Chapter Seven

1. Christopher Fry, "Comedy," *Comedy: Meaning and Form,* ed. Robert W. Corrigan (San Francisco: Chandler Publishing Company, 1965) 16.

2. Karen Jo Torjesen, *When Women Were Priests: Women's Leadership in the Early Church and the Scandal of their Subordination in the Rise of Christianity* (New York: Harper San Francisco/Harper Collins Publishers, 1993) 7.

3. Katherine G. Kanta, *Eleusis: Myth, Mysteries, Histories, Museum,* trans. W.W. Phelps (Athens: 1979) 20 and George E. Mylonas, *Eleusis and the Eleusinian Mysteries* (Princeton: Princeton University Press, 1974) 8.

4. Elaine Pagels, *The Gnostic Gospels* (New York: Vintage Books/Random House, 1981) xviii.

5. See John Boswell's *Christianity, Social Tolerance, and Homosexuality: Gay People in Western Europe from the Beginning of the Christian Era to the Fourteenth Century* (Chicago: The University of Chicago Press, 1980).

6. "Crusades," *Encyclopaedia Britannica* (Chicago: William Benton, Publisher, 1970) 828-834.

7. Michael Baigent, Richard Leigh, and Henry Lincoln, *Holy Blood, Holy Grail* (New York: Dell Publishing/Bantam Doubleday, 1983) 49-51.

8. Baigent 56.

9. Baigent 85.

10. Boswell 272.

11. Anne Llewellyn Barstow, *Witchcraze: A New History of the European Witch Hunts* (San Francisco: Pandora/Harper Collins Publishers, 1994) 161, 220.

12. Barstow 161, 22-23, 1, 27-29.

13. See Charlene Spretnak's *The Resurgence of the Real: Body, Nature, and Place in a Hypermodern World* (New York: Routledge, 1999) for her discussion of the present resurgence of knowledge, attitudes, and movements that she sees as "corrective efforts" to the crises brought about by "Modernity." See also Paul H. Ray and Sherry Ruth Anderson's *The Cultural Creatives: How 50 Million People Are Changing the World.*

Chapter Eight

1. Richard Wilhelm, trans. *The I Ching* or *Book of Changes*. Translated into English by Cary F. Baynes (Princeton: Princeton University Press, 1975) 75.
2. Wilhelm lv-lvi, lviii.
3. Wilhelm lvii.
4. Lawlor 14-15.
5. Wilhelm liii.
6. Wilhelm 76.
7. Wilhelm 78, 478.
8. Wilhelm 478.
9. Lawlor 16.
10. Lawlor 16.
11. Lawlor 16-17.
12. Lawlor 17.
13. Versluis 60-61.
14. Versluis 60-65.
15. See "The First Letter of John," *The Oxford Annotated Bible: Revised Standard Version*, eds. Herbert G. May and Bruce M. Metzger (New York: Oxford University Press, Inc., 1962) 1482.

Chapter Nine

1. C.G. Jung, *Memories, Dreams, Reflections*, ed. Aniela Jaffé, trans. Richard and Clara Winston (New York: Vintage Books/Random House, Inc., 1963) 177.

Chapter Ten

1. Caponigri 170.

2. Max Pulver, "Jesus' Round Dance and Crucifixion According to the Acts of St. John," trans. Ralph Manheim, *The Mysteries: Papers from The Eranos Yearbooks 2*, ed. Joseph Campbell (Princeton: Princeton University Press, 1971) 174-177.

3. "The Gospel of Thomas," *The Nag Hammadi Library*, in English, general ed. James M. Robinson, trans. Members of The Coptic Gnostic Library Project of The Institute for Antiquity and Christianity (San Francisco: Harper & Row, Publishers, 1977) 119, 129.

4. Wilhelm 476.

5. Wilhelm 481.

6. Ronald S. Miller, "Mind and the New Physics/Taking a Quantum Leap in Consciousness: An Interview with Fred Alan Wolf, Ph.D." *Science of Mind* Oct. 1985: 85, 81.

ORGANIZATIONS FOR GLOBAL CHANGE

Cultural Creatives

Tracks, defines, and makes visible the millions of people around the globe who are creating a new worldview and a new culture.

www.culturalcreatives.org

Bioneers: Visionary and Practical Solutions for Restoring the Earth

Provides a directory of resources for diverse, imaginative and practical approaches to restoring the earth.

www.bioneers.org

The Institute of Noetic Sciences (IONS)

A scientific, educational, research organization. Explores the relationship between consciousness and the physical world. Works with researchers in various fields to broaden our understanding of human potential.

www.noetic.org

The Club of Budapest

Presents a vision for a new planetary consciousness and explores practical steps to help us develop global responsibility.

http://www.clubofbudapest.org

The Club of Rome

A global think tank of experts from every continent committed to planetary responsibility on the individual, corporate, and collective levels.

www.ClubOfRome.org

The Berkana Institute

A scientific, educational, research foundation that applies knowledge of living systems to the development of human organizations.

www.berkana.org

Pioneers of Change

A group of young people in their twenties and thirties from all walks of life devoted to bringing about global change by working locally.

www.pioneersofchange.net

The Institute of HeartMath

A research and educational organization. Studies the physiological processes by which the heart communicates with the brain to influence thinking, perception, health, and behavior. Provides strategies for heightened learning skills and violence reduction.

www.heartmath.org

Context Institute

A research organization working toward a global humane and sustainable culture.

www.context.org

Fetzer Institute

Contributes $17 million each year to research, education, and service projects. Explores how the sacredness of life can be integrated into our everyday experience. Tracks and supports small gains that move us toward a healthy, diverse, and whole culture.

www.fetzer.org

New Dimensions World Broadcasting Network

Committed to using the media to serve humanity's highest goals of expanding consciousness and creating a just, meaningful, and balanced world.

www.newdimensions.org

WORKS CITED

Abraham, Ralph. *Chaos, Gaia, Eros: A Chaos Pioneer Uncovers the Three Great Streams of History.* San Francisco: Harper San Francisco/Harper Collins Publishers, 1994.

Baigent, Michael, Richard Leigh, and Henry Lincoln. *Holy Blood, Holy Grail.* New York: Dell Publishing/Bantam Doubleday, 1983.

Barstow, Anne Llewellyn. *Witchcraze: A New History of the European Witch Hunts.* San Francisco: Pandora/Harper Collins Publishers, 1994.

Boswell, John. *Christianity, Social Tolerance, and Homosexuality: Gay People in Western Europe from the Beginning of the Christian Era to the Fourteenth Century.* Chicago: The University of Chicago Press, 1980.

Caponigri, A. Robert. *Time and Idea: The Theory of History in Giambattista Vico.* London: Routledge and Kegan Paul Ltd., 1953.

Chaudhuri, Haridas. *California Institute of Integral Studies: Fall 98 Public Programs.* San Francisco: CIIS, 1998: 25.

"Crusades," *Encyclopaedia Britannica.* Chicago: William Benton, Publisher, 1970: 828-834.

Dechend, Hertha von, and Giorgio de Santillana. *Hamlet's Mill: An Essay on Myth and the Frame of Time.* Boston: Gambit, 1969.

Eisler, Riane. *The Chalice and the Blade: Our History, Our Future.* San Francisco: Harper & Row, Publishers, 1987.

Fry, Christopher. "Comedy," *Comedy: Meaning and Form.* Edited by Robert W. Corrigan. San Francisco: Chandler Publishing Company, 1965.

Goethe, Johann Wolfgang von. *Goethes Werke.* Textkritisch durchgesehen und kommentiert von Erich Trunz. Band 1. München: Verlag C.H. Beck, 1974.

Goswami, Amit, Richard E. Reed, and Maggie Goswami. *The Self-Aware Universe: how consciousness creates the material world.* New York: Jeremy P. Tarcher/Putnam Book, 1995.

Ions, Veronica. *Egyptian Mythology.* New York: Peter Bedrick Books, 1982.

Jung, C.G. *Memories, Dreams, Reflections.* Translated by Richard and Clara Winston. Edited by Aniela Jaffé. New York: Vintage Books/Random House, Inc., 1963.

Jung, C.G., and C. Kerényi. *Essays on a Science of Mythology: The Myths of the Divine Child and the Divine Maiden.* Translated by R.F.C. Hull. New York: Harper Torch Books/Harper & Row, Publishers, 1963.

Kanta, Katherine G. *Eleusis: Myth, Mysteries, History, Museum.* Translated by W.W. Phelps. Athens: 1979.

Kerényi, C. *Eleusis: Archetypal Image of Mother and Daughter.* Translated by Ralph Manheim. New York: Pantheon Books/Bollingen Foundation, 1967.

Kovács, Betty J. "The Return of the Goddess Creatrix in German Romanticism: A Challenge to the Masculine Trinity of Western Consciousness," Diss., University of California, Irvine, 1987.

—. "Journey of the Mothers," *Earthwalking Sky Dancers: Women's Pilgrimages to Sacred Places.* Edited by Leila Castle. Berkeley: Frog, Ltd., 1996.

Laing, R.D. *The Politics of Experience.* New York: Pantheon Books, 1967.

Langer, Susanne K. "On Cassirer's Theory of Language and Myth," *The Philosophy of Ernst Cassirer*. Edited by Paul Arthur Schilpp. La Salle: Open Court Publishing Company, 1973.

Laszlo, Ervin, Stanislav Grof, and Peter Russell. *The Consciousness Revolution: A Transatlantic Dialogue*. Edited by Ervin Laszlo. Boston: Element Books, Inc., 1999.

Matthews, Caitlín. "The Voices of the Wells: Celtic Oral Themes in Grail Literature," *At the Table of the Grail*. Edited by John Matthews. London: Watkins Publishing, 2002.

May, Herbert G., and Bruce M. Metzger, editors. "The First Letter of John," *The Oxford Annotated Bible: Revised Standard Version*. New York: Oxford University Press, Inc., 1962.

Miller, Ronald S. "Mind and the New Physics/Taking a Quantum Leap in Consciousness: An Interview with Fred Alan Wolf, Ph.D.," *Science of Mind* Oct. 1985: 10-14, 81-88.

Mylonas, George E. *Eleusis and the Eleusinian Mysteries*. Princeton: Princeton University Press, 1974.

Newberg, Andrew, Eugene d'Aquili, and Vince Rause. *Why God Won't Go Away: Brain Science and the Biology of Belief*. New York: Ballantine Books/Random House, Inc., 2001.

Pagels, Elaine. *The Gnostic Gospels*. New York: Vintage Books/Random House, 1981.

Pulver, Max. "Jesus' Round Dance and Crucifixion According to the Acts of St. John," *The Mysteries: Papers from the Eranos Yearbooks 2*. Translated by Ralph Manheim and R.F.C. Hull. Edited by Joseph Campbell. Princeton: Princeton University Press, 1971.

Rause, Vince. "The Biology of Belief," *Los Angeles Times Magazine* July 15, 2001: 10-13, 33-35.

Ray, Paul H., and Sherry Ruth Anderson. *The Cultural Creatives: How 50 Million People Are Changing the World.* New York: Harmony Books/Random House, Inc., 2000.

Rilke, Rainer Maria. *Briefe an einen jungen Dichter.* Leipzig: Insel-Verlag, 1932.

Robinson, James M., general editor. *The Nag Hammadi Library,* in English. Translated by Members of The Coptic Gnostic Library Project of The Institute for Antiquity and Christianity. San Francisco: Harper & Row, Publishers, 1977.

Schwaller de Lubicz, R.A. *Symbol and the Symbolic: Egypt, Science and the Evolution of Consciousness.* Translated by Robert and Deborah Lawlor. Brookline: Autumn Press/Random House, Inc., 1978.

Schwartz, Gary E.R., and Linda G.S. Russek. *The Living Energy Universe: a fundamental discovery that transforms science and medicine.* Charlottesville: Hampton Roads Publishing Company, Inc., 1999.

Skafte, Dianne. *Listening to the Oracle: The Ancient Art of Finding Guidance in the Signs and Symbols All Around Us.* New York: Harper San Francisco/Harper Collins Publishers, 1997.

Spretnak, Charlene. *The Resurgence of the Real: Body, Nature, and Place in a Hypermodern World.* New York: Routledge, 1999.

Stace, Walter T., editor. *The Teachings of the Mystics: Selections from the Great Mystics and Mystical Writings of the World.* New York: Mentor Books/The New American Library of World Literature, Inc., 1960.

Strömberg, Gustaf. *The Soul of the Universe.* North Hollywood: Educational Research Institute, 1965.

Swimme, Brian. *The Hidden Heart of the Cosmos: Humanity and the New Story.* Maryknoll: Orbis Books, 1996.

Thompson, William Irwin. *Imaginary Landscape: Making Worlds of Myth and Science.* New York: St. Martin's Press, 1989.

Torjesen, Karen Jo. *When Women Were Priests: Women's Leadership in the Early Church and the Scandal of their Subordination in the Rise of Christianity.* New York: Harper San Francisco/Harper Collins Publishers, 1993.

Versluis, Arthur. *The Egyptian Mysteries.* New York: Arkana/Routledge, 1988.

West, John Anthony. *Serpent in the Sky: The High Wisdom of Ancient Egypt.* Wheaton: The Theosophical Publishing House, 1993.

Wilhelm, Richard, translator. *The I Ching* or *Book of Changes.* Translated into English by Cary F. Baynes. Princeton: Princeton University Press, 1975.

FURTHER READING

Abraham, Ralph, Terence McKenna, and Rupert Sheldrake. *Trialogues at the Edge of the West: Chaos, Creativity, and the Resacralization of the World.* Santa Fe: Bear & Company Publishing, 1992.

Albright, Carol Rausch, and James B. Ashbrook. *Where God Lives in the Human Brain.* Naperville: Sourcebooks, Inc., 2001.

Berry, Thomas. *The Dream of the Earth.* San Francisco: Sierra Club Books, 1988.

Bolen, Jean Shinoda. *Goddesses in Older Women: Archetypes in Women Over 50.* New York: Harper Collins Publishers, Inc., 2001.

Capra, Fritjof. *The Turning Point: Science, Society, and the Rising Culture.* Toronto: Bantam Books, 1988.

—. *The Web of Life: A New Scientific Understanding of Living Systems.* New York: Anchor Books/Doubleday, 1996.

—. *The Tao of Physics: An Exploration of the Parallels Between Modern Physics and Eastern Mysticism.* Boston: Shambhala Publications, Inc., 1999.

Chodorow, Joan, editor. *Encountering Jung: Jung on Active Imagination.* Princeton: Princeton University Press, 1997.

Dossey, Larry. *Reinventing Medicine: Beyond Mind-Body to a New Era of Healing.* San Francisco: Harper San Francisco/Harper Collins Publishers, 1999.

—. *Healing Beyond the Body: Medicine and the Infinite Reach of the Mind.* Boston: Shambhala Publications, Inc., 2001.

Eadie, Betty J. with Curtis Taylor. *Embraced By The Light.* Placerville: Gold Leaf Press, 1992.

Grof, Christina, and Stanislav Grof. *The Stormy Search for the Self: A Guide to Personal Growth through Transformational Crisis.* Los Angeles: Jeremy P. Tarcher, Inc., 1990.

Harman, Willis W., and Elisabet Sahtouris. *Biology Revisioned.* Berkeley: North Atlantic Books, 1998.

—. *Global Mind Change: The Promise of the 21st Century.* 2nd ed. San Francisco: Berrett-Koehler Publishers, Inc., 1998.

Hock, Dee. *Birth of the Chaordic Age.* San Francisco: Berrett-Koehler Publishers, Inc., 1999.

Houston, Jean. *Jump Time: Shaping Your Future in a World of Radical Change.* New York: Jeremy P. Tarcher/Putnam, 2000.

Huxley, Aldous. *The Perennial Philosophy.* New York: Perennial Library/Harper & Row, Publishers, 1945.

James, William. *The Varieties of Religious Experience: A Study in Human Nature.* New York: Collier Books/Macmillan Publishing Company, 1961.

Jung, Carl G., et al. *Man and His Symbols.* Edited by Carl G. Jung, M.-L. von Franz, and John Freeman. Garden City: Doubleday & Company, Inc., 1969.

Krippner, Stanley. "The Epistemology and Technologies of Shamanic States of Consciousness," *Journal for Consciousness Studies.* Vol. 7, No. 11-12, Nov.-Dec. 2000: 93-118.

Laszlo, Ervin. *The Whispering Pond: A Personal Guide to the Emerging Vision of Science.* Rockport: Element Books, Inc., 1996.

—. *Macroshift: Navigating the Transformation to a Sustainable World.* San Francisco: Berrett-Koehler Publishers, Inc., 2001.

Main, Roderick, editor. *Encountering Jung: Jung on Synchronicity and the Paranormal.* Princeton: Princeton University Press, 1998.

Martin, Joel, and Patricia Romanowski. *Love Beyond Life: The Healing Power of After-Death Communications.* New York: Harper Collins Publishers, 1997.

Moody, Jr., Raymond A. *Life After Life: The Investigation of a Phenomenon – Survival of Bodily Death.* Marietta: Mockingbird Books, 1975.

Morse, Melvin with Paul Perry. *Parting Visions: Uses and Meanings of Pre-Death, Psychic, and Spiritual Experiences.* New York: Villard Books, 1994.

Narby, Jeremy. *The Cosmic Serpent: DNA and the Origins of Knowledge.* New York: Jeremy P. Tarcher/Putnam, 1998.

Pearce, Joseph Chilton. *The Biology of Transcendence: A Blueprint of the Human Spirit.* Rochester: Park Street Press, 2002.

Pert, Candace B. *Molecules of Emotion: The Science Behind Mind-Body Medicine.* New York: Touchstone/Simon & Schuster Inc., 1997.

Ring, Kenneth, and Evelyn Elsaesser Valarino. *Lessons from the Light: What We Can Learn from the Near-Death Experience.* Portsmouth: Moment Point Press, Inc., 2000.

Russell, Peter. *Waking Up in Time: Finding Inner Peace in Times of Accelerating Change.* Novato: Origin Press, Inc., 1992.

—. *The Global Brain Awakens: Our Next Evolutionary Leap.* Palo Alto: Global Brain Inc., 1995.

—. *From Science to God: The Mystery of Consciousness and the Meaning of Light.* Las Vegas: Elf Rock Productions, 2001.

Segal, Robert A., editor. *Encountering Jung: Jung on Mythology.* Princeton: Princeton University Press, 1998.

Talbot, Michael. *The Holographic Universe.* New York: Harper Collins Publishers, 1991.

—. *Mysticism and the New Physics.* New York: Arkana/The Penguin Group, 1993.

Thompson, William Irwin, editor. *GAIA 2 Emergence: The New Science of Becoming.* Hudson: Lindisfarne Press, 1991.

Wheatley, Margaret J. *Leadership and the New Science: Discovering Order in a Chaotic World.* 2nd ed. San Francisco: Berrett-Koehler Publishers, Inc., 1999.

Wilber, Ken. *The Marriage of Sense and Soul: Integrating Science and Religion.* New York: Random House, Inc., 1998.

Wolf, Fred Alan. *Parallel Universes: The Search for Other Worlds.* New York: Touchstone/Simon & Schuster Inc., 1990.

—. *The Eagle's Quest: A Physicist's Search for Truth in the Heart of the Shamanic World.* New York: Summit Books/Simon & Schuster Inc., 1991.

—. *The Spiritual Universe: One Physicist's Vision of Spirit, Soul, Matter, and Self.* Portsmouth: Moment Point Press, Inc., 1999.

—. *Mind into Matter: A New Alchemy of Science and Spirit.* Portsmouth: Moment Point Press, Inc., 2001.

Yates, Jenny L., editor. *Encountering Jung: Jung on Death and Immortality*. Princeton: Princeton University Press, 1999.

Zukav, Gary. *The Dancing Wu Li Masters: An Overview of the New Physics*. New York: William Morrow and Company, Inc., 1979.

—. *Soul Stories*. New York: Simon & Schuster Inc., 2000.

Zukav, Gary, and Linda Francis. *The Heart of the Soul: Emotional Awareness*. New York: A Fireside Book/ Simon & Schuster Inc., 2002.

APPENDIX
Dreams/Visions

BETTY'S

Page	Date	Description
21	11/91	"Are you ready? A miracle, a miracle."
33-34	08/25/91	Chaco Canyon/World Child
39-40	1971	Painting dream/Pregnant with Pisti
41-42	10/17/89	Civil War/The Dead Live
44	03/17/91	Egyptian Jackal/Anubis
47	07/12/91	Intruder/Rapist
48	07/30/91	News of Pisti's death
49	08/21/91	Expansive Energy/Souls from nonmaterial dimension
50	09/01/91	Expansive Energy/Other World
50-51	10/23/91	World Catastrophe/Round Dance
53-54	10/28/91	Expansive Energy/Soul from another dimension/We are entering into project together
66-67	11/91	Milky Way
72-73	1989	"We can do nothing but create."
88-90	12/91	Surfing with Pisti on ocean of life
94	1992	Snake boots
97	1992	Pisti as Trickster Bard/What is real anyway?
106	1992	Perpetrator
107	1989	Addicted to ordinary consciousness
110-111	1992	Death Valley/"It can never be healed!"
114	1992	Birth from Heart/"The Radiant One."
118-119	1992	North Pole/Cauldrons of shit
128-129	10/30/93	Spain/Cathedral V-O-I-D Ritual
131	03/94	Istvan's first appearance/century plant
135	1995	Transparent glass bowl/tomb
136	11/25/89	Sinister Creature/Circle of women
138	12/27/93	Called to brother in the name of dead husband
138	1993	Istvan leaves/dies
146-147	1994	Experienced Istvan's accident
151-155	1990	Disk of light, consciousness and love

155	1990	Budapest/Sacred stones
161	1992	Doubt absorbs light
164-166	05/23/92	"Spirit and Matter are One."

~

ISTVAN'S

Page	Date	Description
19-20	11/91	Trauma Center/Pisti as bridge
28	10/91	Pisti's accident /"Dad, I will be out of the house for a little while."
60-64	11/91	Twins/Pisti holding earth
95-97	1992	Film of Universes/New Child/New DNA
115-118	06/92	*The I Ching*/ML
138-139	03/16/92	First vision of death
140-141	09/19/92	Death
142	11/10/93	Death
143-144	02/19/94	Death
146	05/92	Meeting Pisti or "look-alike"
160-161	03/16/92	Points of Light/Love on the earth

~

PISTI'S

Page	Date	Description
29-30	1983	Death in Trauma Center/Eternal Circle of Light
34	1990	"Protect everything that is coming into being."
55-57	1991	Death and Return to the Light (Chorus)
162-163	1990 or 1991	Out-of-body experience/Working to create a balanced world

~

JENNY'S

Page	Date	Description
92	1992	Pisti/the earth
167	03/03/94 (Early morning)	Powerful energy in room

~

PAUL'S

Page	Date	Description
147-148	1994	Szentes/Istvan and Pisti

INDEX

G

H

I

J

K

L

M

N

O

P

Q

R

S

About the Author

Betty J. Kovács received her Ph.D. from the University of California, Irvine, in Comparative Literature and Theory of Symbolic/Mythic Language. She has studied and taught in Europe and the United States. She taught Literature, Writing, and Symbolic/Mythic Language for twenty-five years. She served many years as Chair and Program Chair on the Board of Directors of the Jung Society of Claremont in California and sits on the Academic Advisory Board of Forever Family Foundation. She is author of *Merchants of Light: The Consciousness That Is Changing the World,* winner of the Nautilus Silver Book Award and The Scientific & Medical Network 2019 Book Prize.

Contact Betty Kovács at bjkovacs@earthlink.net.
Visit www.kamlak.com for a complete list of her work.

Print and ebooks available from local and online bookstores/ libraries and from the publisher.